THE AHWAHNEE

YOSEMITE'S GRAND HOTEL

by Keith S. Walklet

DNC Parks & Resorts at Yosemite, Inc.
and Yosemite Association
Yosemite National Park, California

Coordinated by Steven Medley
Design by Sandy Bell Design,
Springdale, Utah
Printed in Singapore

Produced by the Yosemite
Association.

All color photographs by Keith S.
Walklet, unless otherwise noted.
Historic photographs courtesy of
the Yosemite Research Library,
unless otherwise noted.

Delaware North Companies
PARKS & RESORTS

YOSEMITE
ASSOCIATION

FRONT COVER
The Ahwahnee in spring.

BACK COVER
Pacific dogwood blooms in late
April contrast with ponderosa pines
on the wooded grounds of The
Ahwahnee.

INSIDE FRONT AND BACK
COVERS
Details from the *toile pente*, or
painted tapestry, by Robert Boardman Howard in the Mural Room.

PAGE ONE
The Great Lounge as it appears
today.

SOURCES & ACKNOWLEDGMENTS

This book began as a revision of Shirley Sargent's wonderful history, *The Ahwahnee: Yosemite's Classic Hotel*, published in 1977 in honor of the hotel's 50th anniversary. That work contains a wealth of anecdotal information Shirley obtained directly from participants in the hotel's history, and it remains one of the most significant sources of information for Ahwahnee researchers. Three other key documents are *The Ahwahnee*, with its wonderfully detailed description of the hotel's décor, originally prepared by Dr. Phyllis Ackerman and revised at least twice by Mary Curry Tresidder and Jeannette Dyer Spencer; a thorough history of the U.S. Naval Special Hospital by an anonymous author; and a lengthy memo from Don Tresidder to Frederick Law Olmsted, Jr., in 1927. For insight into the genius of the hotel's architect, Gilbert Stanley Underwood, I relied on Joyce Zaitlin's *Underwood: His Spanish Revival, Rustic, Art Deco, Railroad and Federal Architecture*. For a broad perspective on how The Ahwahnee compares with other national park hotels, *Great Lodges of the West* by Christine Barnes is a great source.

One of my goals for this project was to leave a path for other researchers to follow, as there is still more to discover. Because footnotes were considered impractical given the format of this book, I have placed a list of sources, a draft copy of my text, and any new information I unearthed in the Yosemite Research Library. This project is a continuing passion, so I wel-come any information others may have.

Given the frequency with which I spoke to some folks, I might have given the impression that each was the only person I consulted, yet all were generous with their time and knowledge. They include Michael and Jeanne Adams, Anne Adams Helms, Evan Adkins, Keith Alt, James Anile, Lisa Strong-Aufhauser, Kevin Bennett, Mary and Robert Anderson, Brett Archer, Connie Archer, Christine Barnes, Barbara Beroza, Bob Binnewies, Tom Bopp, Tony Brenta, Bruce Brossman, Ginger Burley, Gayanne Famrini, Craig Chase, Ann and Wyatt Creswell, Primo Custudio, Lisa Dapprich, Linda Eade, Don Evans, Ed Finney, Jack Finney, Naomi Arlund Flint, Jack Francis, Andrea Fulton, Brian Grogan, Karen Hales, Margarita Harder, Roland Henin, Rick Hesidence, Jan Herman, Barb and Hank Jaquimet, Dudley Kendall, Tony and Anne Underwood Kulish, Kathy Langley, Laura Lemessurier, Di Marchese, Bob and Nancy Maynard, Dwayne McFann, Sharon McQueen, Julie Miller, Martha Miller, John ONeill, Greg Owens, Julia Parker, Sandon Patterson, Joyce Perkins, Debbie Price, Mike Quinn, Leroy Radanovich, Petra Rehorova, Steve Roller, Gene Rose, Bill Rust, Lee Shackleton, Karen Shanower, Ed Shields, DeeDee Smith, Don Snooty, Jim Snyder, Susan Snyder, Jan Stipula, Jim and Kim Tucker, Bill Tiscornia, Jane Usher, Tamara Weil-Hearon, and Joyce Zaitlin.

My thanks go to Kevin Kelly, western regional vice-president for DNC Parks & Resorts, and Greg Owens of the company's retail department for the invitation to undertake this project, and to Steve Medley for offering his editing skills and the expertise of the Yosemite Association to ensure that the publication would be of the highest quality. Linda Eade in the Yosemite Research Library was an enthusiastic partner in this archeological expedition, and designer Sandy Bell deserves accolades for transforming my piles of art and text into a beauti-ful book. Thanks, too, to Joe Levine and Rebecca Baier at Calypso Imaging for careful and speedy processing of my film.

And finally, special thanks go to Glenn Crosby, the ultimate host, cook, and formidable Scrabble opponent, without whose assistance this project never would have happened.

This book is dedicated to Shirley Sargent, Yosemite historian and author, on whose shoulders we all stand.

CONTENTS

COLOR DETAILS
Selected stained glass details are from the five-by-six-foot windows designed by Jeannette Dyer Spencer for the Great Lounge. Each window contains a different pattern based on Native American designs. Photographs by Leroy Radanovich, DNC.

BACKGROUND
One of the floor-to-ceiling windows in the Great Lounge with the top stained glass window designed by Jeannette Dyer Spencer. Photograph by Ansel Adams, YP&CCo. Collection.

I suppose the fact that I wasn't impressed with The Ahwahnee when I first saw it makes me the ideal person to boast of its beauty. For who is more sincere than a skeptic?

It is true that after constant prompting from my new friends and co-workers in Yosemite in the autumn of 1984, I finally wandered from my humble tent cabin down the cul-de-sac at the base of the Royal Arches, past the stone gatehouse, by the massive boulders and sequoia-lined parking lot, to the wooden walkway and into the lobby. It was a long walk for someone with a prejudiced chip on his shoulder.

The sounds of my footsteps mixed with those of others in the dim light of the hotel's great halls, but I remained apart. It was nice, I remember thinking, but not nearly so impressive as my first love, the Old Faithful Inn in Yellowstone. My visit was brief. I wandered to the elevator lobby, took a quick glance at the Great Lounge, and left without even seeing the dining room. What is all the fuss about, I wondered?

Nearly twenty years later, I chuckle at my naiveté for I have grown to appreciate this building with a shameless passion developed by spending countless hours in the light of the stained glass windows of the Great Lounge, holding hands by candlelight in an intimate corner of the immense dining room, and having my entire being sail among the lofty granite walls of Yosemite Valley as the soloists spill out their hearts for the Bracebridge Dinner's highlight, "O Holy Night." When I run my fingers across the hand-wrought iron railings, breathe in the fragrance of a

wood fire, and ease into one of the Beacon chairs in the Great Lounge, I am home.

Researching the history of the hotel has strengthened those feelings, for in the collections of official Yosemite Park & Curry Company and NPS memos, in the faded photographs and newspaper clippings found in the Yosemite Research Library, and in my countless conversations with employees, I became aware of the deep desire shared by each

ABOVE
The floral-patterned fabric of the chairs in the Mural Room complements the hammered copper fireplace and the colors and design of the *toile pente* by Robert Boardman Howard.

OPPOSITE
A stately black oak frames the south façade of The Ahwahnee.

INTRODUCTION

and every person involved in the hotel's planning, construction, decoration, and operation. They all wanted this hotel to be the finest that could possibly be built. Their success is reflected in the fact that, like Yosemite's magnificent landscape, the hotel serves as a reminder of the rewards that await those with the inspiration to reach beyond the ordinary.

So it is a great honor to have the opportunity with this volume to share the wonder I have for this magnificent structure and the visionaries whose remarkable talent it embodies. I'm in love with The Ahwahnee, and by the conclusion of this book, I sincerely hope you will be, too.

Keith S. Walklet, Boise, Idaho
November, 2003

THE ORIGIN OF AN IDEA

For years it has been suggested that the major impetus for building The Ahwahnee hotel was a brief visit to Yosemite in the 1920s by American-born Lady Astor, England's first female Member of Parliament. As the story goes, the good lady left in a huff after getting a look at Yosemite Valley's top-of-the-line accommodations in the Sentinel Hotel. The 50-plus-year-old property's drafty rooms and community bathroom reputedly were not up to her standards. When Stephen T. Mather, the first Director of the National Park Service, got wind of her indignation, he, the story concludes, determined to build a luxury hotel suitable for individuals of wealth and influence, who would in turn become supporters of the national park system.

Given that The Ahwahnee was nearly completed by the time of Lady Astor's visit, her indignation could not have been the prime motivation for building the hotel. Prior to the July 14, 1927 opening of The Ahwahnee, however, the scenario described might have been repeated by any number of "travelers of wealth and means" who chanced a visit to Yosemite. Director Mather made it his per-

sonal mission to see that members of this touring class could be appropriately accommodated in the parks, including Yosemite. He set out to develop the "national park brand," which in his mind would associate the finest scenery with the finest roads, restaurants, and hotels.

Mather's Vision

The park "system" that Mather inherited in 1915 had no central governing body, occasional funding, and inconsistent facilities and services. The landscapes were rich with wildlife, pristine lakes, and lofty peaks, but the budget for the sixteen national parks and twenty-one national monuments at the time the park service was established in 1916 was only $19,500.

Mather believed that the decision-makers who had the potential to offer support at the highest levels of government were not interested in a primitive camping or hostelling experience when they visited the parks. Each of the parks, he reasoned, should have a quality place for guests to gather, dine, and rest—a location, fitting in with the park surroundings, to serve as the centerpiece for their visit. He observed, "Scenery is a hollow enjoyment to a tourist who sets out in the morning after an indigestible breakfast and a fitful sleep on an impossible bed."

Many of the national parks already had grand hotels. At Yellowstone it was the Old Faithful Inn, and at Glacier the Many

> "Scenery is a hollow enjoyment to a tourist who sets out in the morning after an indigestible breakfast and a fitful sleep on an impossible bed." —STEPHEN T. MATHER

BELOW
Cramped campgrounds forced visitors so closely together that they could sometimes share tent pegs, and such crowded conditions persisted into the 1950s.

BACKGROUND
From all accounts, winter conditions inside Yosemite's "premier accommodations," the Sentinel Hotel, weren't much better than what these adventurous women experienced outside—the buildings shared bath facilities and drafty rooms were considered sub-par by Stephen Mather, Director of the National Parks.

ABOVE
Built inn 1888, the Stoneman House was the first "luxury" hotel built in Yosemite. It operated just eight years before fire destroyed it, a fate that befell numerous early park hotels.

Glaciers Hotel. The Grand Canyon was known for the El Tovar. Most of these properties had been built by the railroads to serve their passengers. But Yosemite, known to be Mather's favorite park of all, had none.

Tourist accommodations in Yosemite had never approached the quality of those in similarly spectacular locations in Europe and in other parks. An early attempt at a luxury hotel, the Stoneman House, burned in 1896, and park superintendents regularly urged that a replacement be built.

Playing to the Audience

In 1915, the Panama Pacific Exposition was held in San Francisco to celebrate the completion of the Panama Canal. Mather saw the exposition's audience as exactly the type of people he wanted to lure to the parks. To capture the interest of those in attendance at the Panama Canal event, the new director organized the third National Parks Conference on the campus of the University of California at Berkeley (his alma mater) at the same time the exposition was held in March. Discussion topics at the conference included improving access to the national parks with better roads, improving the quality of the accommodations in the parks, and the operation of park concessions as regulated monopolies.

While hosting the conference, Mather had several agendas. "For a curtain-raiser to his parks administration," his biographer recounts, "he wanted to make some noise—preferably in Yosemite." His "loudest" actions were to propose the purchase of the Tioga Road, Yosemite's old trans-Sierra mining route, and then to prevail upon his friends and successful businessmen to provide funds to do so. He quickly obtained commitments from his associates for half the asking price, and he came up with the rest from his own pocket.

The acquisition and improvement of the Tioga Road, at the time the only practical auto route over the Sierra between Sonora Pass and Bakersfield, was both tangible and symbolic proof of his commitment to improved access to the park. Enhancing the accommodations proved to be a much more complex task. Even without the publicity that came with buying highways, Mather knew that facilities in Yosemite Valley in 1915 were likely to be overrun by the crowds attending the exposition. He made it known that he was also seeking someone with the financial wherewithal to start up a new Yosemite concession that summer, to eventually build a modern hotel.

Looking for a Hotel Builder

While at the Panama Pacific Exposition, Mather met D. J. Desmond, a well-financed Southern California caterer who contracted food service at construction sites. Desmond arranged for a contractor to convert the former military barracks on the present-day location of Yosemite Lodge into a lounge and dining room, and purchased some additional prefabricated cabins to augment the site's 156 tent platforms. The instant camp was ready for guests by June 12, 1915.

ABOVE
Jennie and David Curry, with Jennie's father, Robert Foster, at Camp Curry, circa 1904.

BELOW
Donald Tressider, president of Yosemite Park and Curry Co., gives an address at the cornerstone laying of the still-unnamed Ahwahnee on August 1, 1926. In front row, from left to right, NPS Director Stephen T. Mather, A. B. C. Dohrmann, and Jennie Curry.

Mather next turned to Desmond for long-term solutions. The Desmond Park Service Company committed to a 1916 contract that required it to build a modern, fireproof hotel on the valley floor by the following year. In September, Desmond's ascent to power was confirmed when the U.S. Secretary of the Interior announced the plan to initiate the regulated monopoly concept in Yosemite with Desmond as the primary operator.

Unfortunately for Mather, Desmond was a disappointment. In 1916, he stretched his capital to the limit as he constructed new facilities at Merced Lake, Tenaya Lake, and Tuolumne Meadows (eventually known as High Sierra Camps), and started work on a three-story hotel at Glacier Point. The furthest he got with a luxury facility was the digging of the basement for the upscale "Grizzly Hotel" in Yosemite Valley. The tight conditions of a wartime economy and his own financial extravagances caught up with him a year later. Bankrupt, he collapsed in nervous exhaustion. His company was reorganized by its primary stockholders to become the Yosemite National Park Company.

Desmond's main competitor was the well-established Curry Camping Company. Its owner, David Curry, and his wife Jenny had a successful business selling low-priced accommodations in Yosemite Valley. Rancor developed between the two concessioners, and at times it was severe. Things calmed down considerably with Desmond's bankruptcy and David Curry's death in 1917. Still, neither of the two hotel companies seemed to have the wherewithal to develop the quality accommodations that Mather dreamed about.

The Yosemite Park & Curry Company

Mather decided a joint venture was the path to the future of concessions in Yosemite. In 1924, Hubert Work, the incoming Secretary of the Interior, commanded that the two competitors merge or vacate. Not surprisingly, they elected to merge. In May of 1925, the officers of the newly formed entity, Yosemite Park and Curry Co. (YP&CCo.), signed a 20-year contract with the Interior Department allowing the company a regulated monopoly on services in Yosemite Valley and requiring it to build a modern, fireproof hotel.

Harry Chandler, publisher of the *Los Angeles Times*, was at the top of the list of notables on the Board of Directors guiding the new company. YP&CCo.'s first president, Donald Tresidder, had risen in the ranks of the Curry Camping Company and wed David and Jenny's daughter, Mary. Personable and articulate, Tresidder proved to be an able leader.

The YP&CCo. officers approached their assignment to build a luxury hotel with a sober sense of duty. A site for the building had been selected and staked out in 1924, and an architect was hired in July of 1925. The merger of the two concession operations was finalized that November. Mather's long wait for appropriate lodgings in Yosemite was near an end.

HISTORY OF THE SITE

The site of Yosemite's first luxury hotel was used by Native American people for thousands of years. One ancient group of Miwok chose a grassy area just west of the Royal Arches for a permanent village they called *Wis-kah-lah*. There they probably constructed (for assembly and dancing) a central ceremonial house, which was surrounded by family dwellings, sweathouses, and acorn granaries called *chuck-ahs*.

Yosemite Valley was known to them as "Ahwahnee" or "place of the gaping mouth," and they called themselves the Ahwahneechee. The Ahwahneechee were skilled hunters and gatherers whose primary staple was acorns. Their impact on the land was slight, the only visible long-term evidence of their presence being mortar holes worn in granite slabs by the process of grinding acorns.

Located on the sunny north side, *Wis-kah-lah* was similar to the majority of over thirty other encampments archeologists have identified in Yosemite Valley. Oak trees were abundant, and the meadows were a good source of willow and hemp for baskets. A short stroll to the south, the Merced River provided an ample supply of water through the driest of summers.

The discovery of gold in California and the resulting rush for riches brought an influx of Europeans to the region and a painful end to the Native Americans' longstanding lifestyle. The secluded and rugged nature of Yosemite Valley initially insulated the tribe from conflict, but as the

> "Indians walk softly and hurt the landscape hardly more than the birds and squirrels, and their brush and bark huts last hardly longer than those of wood rats, while their more enduring monuments vanish in a few centuries."
>
> —JOHN MUIR

fortune seekers pushed deeper into the mountains in pursuit of ore, altercations occurred. When a frustrated group of Indians attacked a trading post in the Merced River Canyon, its owner James Savage successfully appealed to the new governor of California to allow him to assemble a battalion of volunteers to track them down.

In March of 1851, while in pursuit of the Native Americans, this loose-knit vigilante group became the first Europeans to enter and explore Yosemite Valley. One battalion member, Lafayette H. Bunnell, was moved by the powerful scenery and significance of the human drama that the forced removal of the Miwok people represented. Thinking that they

TOP AND BACKGROUND
Details from a Hupa storage basket in The Ahwahnee collection show exceptional artistry.

TOP MIDDLE
Detail from a Yokuts mush basket in The Ahwahnee collection.

ABOVE
Centuries before Europeans first entered Yosemite Valley, Native Americans found the site where The Ahwahnee is built to be an ideal location for a village. Grinding rocks mark the spots adjacent to the hotel parking lot where the prized acorns were transformed into the main ingredient of a nutritious porridge.

Kenneyville, a large stables business on the site of The Ahwahnee, shown at the turn of the twentieth century.

The three-story Glacier Point Hotel was built by D. J. Desmond and the Yosemite National Park Company in 1917. While it offered an amazing view, the hotel was rather rustic. It burned down in 1969.

called themselves the Yosemites, Bunnell suggested that the valley be named in tribute to its former residents.

About 1867, James C. Lamon settled at the former location of *Wis-ka-lah*, homesteading 379 acres upon which he built a cabin in 1869. An adventurous and industrious man, Lamon reputedly was the first European to intentionally overwinter in Yosemite Valley. By 1870, Royal Arch Farm, as he called it, featured crops of blackberries, raspberries, and strawberries, and orchards of apple, almond, peach, pear, and plum trees, many of which still bear fruit today.

Lamon died in 1877, and his homestead was leased by Aaron Harris, who fenced off the adjacent meadow to the west to raise fodder for travelers' livestock. Within a year, Harris converted the farm into Yosemite Valley's first formal campground.

When fire destroyed the building that Harris used as a camp store a decade later, he left the valley. The property was leased by the state commissioners to William F. Coffman and George W. Kenney for a livery operation. Kenneyville, as the stables operation came to be known, thrived for over a quarter-century until the increased popularity of automobiles diminished the need for horses.

With the business reduced to little more than a saddle-horse operation by the 1920s, the relatively isolated site was a natural choice when the National Park Service and Yosemite Park and Curry Company were considering where to build the new "All-Year Hotel."

ALL-YEAR ACCESS

Between 1915 and 1920, the automobile revolutionized the nature of travel, displacing carriages and horses practically overnight. Stephen Mather was probably one of the first to trade in his buggy for a horseless carriage. With nearly a million cars being added to the country's roads in 1915 alone, it was inevitable that increasing numbers of automobiles would visit the national parks. Yosemite's travel statistics bear this out, with visitation increasing from 15,154 in 1915 to 68,906 in 1920.

Mather was doing everything he could to make sure the automobile routes to and within the park were conducive to travel. Until 1926, however, access by car was a fair weather only option, given Yosemite's often snowy winters. A major step to change this situation was taken on August 1 of that year when the All-Year Highway to Yosemite was opened.

California Route 140 climbs through the foothills of the Sierra to Mariposa and Briceburg, then follows the contours of the Merced River Canyon to El Portal and into the park. It is a picturesque road that took six years to build. Unlike the other routes into the park, it never climbs above 3,000 feet in elevation until it reaches Yosemite. From the very first day it opened, it was wildly popular.

The Yosemite superintendent's report shows that on February 13, 1927, some 875 autos made it to Yosemite Valley, compared to only a handful the previous year. The YP&CCo. officials were unprepared for the onslaught. Increases continued all year with the flood of visitors reaching epic proportions on Memorial Day weekend when an estimated 27,000 people descended on the valley. Over 3,000 automobiles were believed to have entered the park each day. By the end of the year, nearly twice as many visitors had entered the park as in the previous year. Mather had lived to see his goal of all-year access to Yosemite achieved. His next objective was to get an all-year hotel opened.

"Why, look at those cars! There must be close to two hundred of them. Where's your imagination man? Some day there'll be a thousand!"

—STEPHEN T. MATHER TO D. J. DESMOND

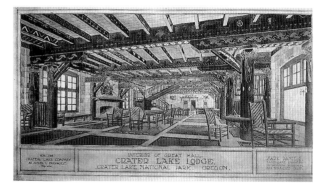

TOP
Mather visited park lodges such as Robert Reamer's Old Faithful Inn in Yellowstone National Park for inspiration.

ABOVE
The rendering of the proposed lobby for the Crater Lake Lodge by Mark Daniels shows remarkable similarities to the decorative design used at The Ahwahnee years later by Jeannette Dyer Spencer. Photograph courtesy of Oregon Historical Society, #Gi C22.

BELOW
A "Chalet" conceived in 1917 by Mark Daniels for his Yosemite Village master plan. Daniel's classic designs employing stone and timber are definitive of appropriate park architecture.

The early failed attempts to secure a luxury hotel for the park provided valuable lessons along with time for the idea to mature, time for park access roads to be improved, and time for the National Park Service to develop some financial and political momentum.

For ideas about what form the grand hotel should take, Stephen Mather crisscrossed the west in 1915, inspecting the parks and the visitor facilities with his trusted assistant, Horace Albright. Their visit to the Glacier Park Hotel and outlying chalets built by Louis Hill of the Northern Pacific Railroad was one source of inspiration and confirmation.

Albright recalls in his autobiography that Mather was fascinated. He loved the chalets and thought

National Park Service, so that he could adapt them to other national parks. Daniels already had been thinking about an overall architectural theme for the parks. A capable artist, he quickly developed conceptual designs for a new village in Yosemite, and began work on plans for Crater Lake, Sequoia, Mount Rainier, and Glacier National Parks.

Daniels echoed Mather's feelings about the need to build quality guest facilities. He advocated "a three-tiered system of accommodations which provided hotels or mountain chalets for overnight lodging, permanent camps where visitors would sleep in tents and take meals in a dining room, and camps where visitors would sleep in tents and cook their own food." This system is essentially what exists in most of the larger parks today.

SEEDS OF INSPIRATION

the main lodge was "the perfect hotel for a national park . . . there was a lobby four stories high with twenty-four giant fir-tree pillars ringing it, huge Indian-design carpets, a buffalo skin tipi, great Japanese lanterns, shops, and other wonders. Then came a dining room to seat two hundred hungry people at a time, waitresses in Swiss costumes, not to mention a swimming pool, [and] a sun parlor with afternoon tea."

Impressed as he was, Mather determined to get the plans immediately from Hill and turn them over to Mark Daniels, then General Superintendent and Landscape Engineer of the

Mark Daniels' contribution to the development of an appropriate architectural style for the national parks is often overlooked. He demonstrated exceptional skill in blending form and function, and considered carefully the placement of the structures in his proposals. While there were existing examples of rustic architecture in the parks, Daniels clearly deserves credit for contributing an overall plan with a consistent tone and aesthetic that eventually became known as "park rustic" architecture.

AN ARCHITECT IS SELECTED

In July of 1925, the Yosemite Park and Curry Co. selected Gilbert Stanley Underwood to design the new "All-Year Hotel." Stephen Mather was fond of assisting up-and-coming professionals, and Underwood had just completed three projects with which Mather was quite pleased. It is likely that Mather suggested that YP&CCo. officials hire the young architect.

Mather and his staff of landscape engineers first took note of Underwood when he submitted concept proposals for a new administrative office and a post office in Yosemite Village. He also had been selected to design lodges at Zion and Bryce National Parks. Underwood's scheme for the administrative offices in the park was rejected, as were his plans for the post office—they were considered too extravagant. Underwood's second concept for the post office was accepted and executed, and when he was tapped to design The Ahwahnee in 1925, the post office and two lodge buildings had been completed.

The head of his own firm at age 35, Underwood had a small frame that made him seem younger than his years. Yet from this diminutive man came ideas that matched the grand vision that Mather had for a first class hotel in his favorite park. With each project that Underwood completed for the NPS, he expanded his architectural vocabulary so that by the time he worked on plans for The Ahwahnee, he was not only fluent in the park design vernacular, but also poetic.

His selection was not entirely without controversy. There was some concern among board members that the distance between Los Angeles and Yosemite would result in inadequate on-site supervision and slow design revisions. Underwood's optimism and enthusiasm won out, however. He told Donald Tresidder that "the Yosemite position offered him the opportunity of his life . . . and, if necessary, he would move his entire office force to Yosemite."

LEFT
Gilbert Stanley Underwood circa 1930s. Photograph courtesy of Ann Underwood Kulish.

BOTTOM
Underwood's 1925 representation of The Ahwahnee depicts a building that blends in with its environment. Note the architect's intended entrance for the hotel at right, a passageway now occupied by The Ahwahnee Lounge. Photograph courtesy of DNC.

BUILDING THE HOTEL

Moving Targets

From the moment he was retained to design The Ahwahnee, Gilbert Stanley Underwood was running behind. Stephen Mather, Horace Albright, Interior Secretary Hubert Work, Donald Tresidder, and members of the YP&CCo. board chose the site for the hotel on April 3, 1925. Underwood signed his one-year contract in July, and the pressure was on to complete the project for Mather's desired Christmas of 1926 opening.

Given Yosemite's remoteness and the board's uncertainty about what it really wanted, the 1926 target proved unrealistic. The principals were overly optimistic about the expected completion date, and numerous problems arose that worked to lengthen the project.

What Underwood was asked to design was a fireproof structure with 100 guest rooms that suited the grandness of Yosemite Valley, and a site plan that allowed for the eventual construction of satellite guest cottages similar to those at Bryce and Zion. The building was to create the feeling of a large home. Commercial activity, including the registration desk, cashier area, and the candy and gift shops, was to be in a separate wing. Tresidder noted that "people desiring such services, need only to be aware of the existence of these units when they had business to transact."

Following a number of alterations to his original plans (including those that relocated bathrooms and moved the kitchen closer to the dining room), Underwood was able to secure the approval to proceed from the National Park Service in late March 1926. Though more changes would follow, the perimeter of the hotel was staked out the following month.

In May, unable to solicit bids from contractors, a concerned Donald Tresidder informed the board that revised plans from Underwood were not likely to be ready until July. With the normal bid process lasting at least three months, he reasoned, construction would commence just as the winter frosts arrived. And if that were the case, the concrete work would need to be delayed until the following spring.

"When victory is won, there are no signs left of the struggle."

—FROM A PROMOTIONAL PAMPHLET FOR AHWAHNEE CONTRACTOR JAMES MACLAUGHLIN

To keep the project moving forward, Tresidder suggested that YP&CCo. forgo the normal bid process and offer the job to a reputable builder on the basis of a flat sum plus salary. James MacLaughlin, a San Francisco contractor who mainly built schools and churches, was recommended for the job by board member John S. Drum, who cited MacLaughlin's honesty, reliability, and ability to come in on budget. YP&CCo. approved the recommendation.

ABOVE
Park Superintendent W. B. Lewis, YP&CCo. Director A. B. C. Dohrmann, NPS Architect Tom Vint, YP&CCo. President Donald Tressider, and Ahwahnee architect Gilbert Stanley Underwood display a rendering of the proposed hotel on its future site (Kenneyville).

OPPOSITE
With Yosemite Falls as a backdrop, the solarium takes shape. The hotel's architect, Gilbert Stanley Underwood, gave specific instructions for the masons to arrange the granite blocks so that only weathered surfaces were visible, ensuring that when completed, the hotel already achieved an aged look. When this photo was taken, the large faux wood (concrete) beams projecting off each column to support the immense exterior lanterns had yet to be installed.

BELOW
When constructed in 1927, The Ahwahnee was to be the cornerstone around which all other Yosemite Park and Curry Company enterprises would center. The plan was to offer "a service for every tourist with prices for every purse." The building's actual cornerstone, placed on August 1, 1926, is located to the left of the wooden walkway just before the doors to the hotel lobby.

ABOVE
Beneath the hotel's shell of concrete and massive granite blocks is a skeleton constructed of 680 tons of structural steel I-beams.

BELOW
All told, 245 laborers, carpenters, and skilled craftsmen worked on the hotel. Their efforts are reflected in a building with an industrial underbelly, but a decidedly hand-crafted appearance.

To the board's relief, MacLaughlin jumped at the opportunity, submitting a bid to complete the monumental task "for a maximum guaranteed cost of $525,000, including our fee"—and he proposed to do so in just six months! Some board members expressed skepticism, questioning whether the drawings provided to MacLaughlin were detailed enough to allow an accurate estimate. So that things could move forward, YP&CCo. agreed to let MacLaughlin pour the foundation of the hotel. When the final plans arrived, he would be given the opportunity to adjust his bid, if appropriate. If the board determined at that point that MacLaughlin's bid was too high, the remainder of the construction could be put out to bid to other contractors.

Most of the materials for the hotel were brought in from outside the park. Shirley Sargent has reported that for thirteen months, seven days per week, a steady stream of six-wheel Fageol trucks (the highly regarded predecessor of the Peterbilt brand) hauled the building supplies up the winding

Merced River Canyon on the new All-Year Highway to the valley construction site. Besides 5,000 tons of building stone, close to 700 tons of structural steel also was imported. The massive timbers used for the dining room trusses were harvested at Hazel Green, just outside the park boundary.

The parade of trucks paused briefly on August 1, when dignitaries gathered to lay the hotel's cornerstone as part of a larger celebration marking the 75th anniversary of the "discovery" of Yosemite Valley and the completion of the All-Year Highway. At that time hopes were still high that the The Ahwahnee would be finished in time for a grand opening at Christmas.

Things bogged down when MacLaughlin work crews caught up to Underwood, who was still struggling to incorporate many changes into his "final" design. Joyce Zaitlin reports that besides the modifications called for by the board, state regulatory agencies concerned with such factors as fire safety hampered quick completion of the construction with bureaucratic delays.

As progress slowed, finger-pointing began in earnest. YP&CCo. blamed MacLaughlin and Underwood, MacLaughlin blamed YP&CCo. and Underwood, and Underwood stood his ground and blamed YP&CCo. and MacLaughlin.

During this rancorous period, the board chose a name for the hotel. John S. Drum moved that the hotel be called The Ahwahnee, and Donald Tresidder, who some suggest collaborated with his wife Mary to come up with the name, seconded the motion. It passed unanimously on October 12, 1926. The new name did nothing to speed the construction, however. Only a month later, frustrated YP&CCo. officials met with counsel to determine a course of action to pressure the architect and builder.

Underwood's contract had expired in July, and the terms under which he continued working are not clear. Tresidder felt that the initial drafting costs had been excessive and recommended that a new contract with a fee based on a fixed percentage of total building cost be arranged. A committee appointed to look into the matter determined it to be inadvisable to negotiate with Underwood until the hotel was completed.

MacLaughlin positioned himself for the approaching legal storm, venting his frustrations and stating his case in a March 18 letter to Tresidder. "It is impossible to complete the construction of the Ahwahnee Hotel under the chaotic conditions created by owners and their agents which have continued since last September ... Already the changes in plans have made a structure so completely different in character, that it is no longer within any contract I have with you." MacLaughlin's irritation was justifiable. Changes to the building since the original contract was signed amounted to a staggering 18,000 additional square feet!

YP&CCo.'s lawyers could see that MacLaughlin's position was a valid one. While the board was dissatisfied with his seemingly loose supervision of the work crews in the winter, they also recognized that their own supervisory efforts had been far from stellar. Counsel proposed three potential courses for the board to consider. First, it could treat MacLaughlin's letter as a breach of contract, fire him, install a new builder to complete the project, and sue MacLaughlin for damages and the excess cost of the building beyond the $525,000 originally quoted. Alternatively, it could arrange for YP&CCo. and MacLaughlin to select their respective arbiters, and use a third party to resolve the dispute. Finally, it could affirm the contract with MacLaughlin, and urge him to proceed toward completion as quickly as possible.

Knowing full well that the final price for the hotel was likely to be over $1 million, the board chose the third option. By the time of the hotel's completion, the cost for construction of The Ahwahnee had grown to $1,225,000.

TOP
YP&CCo. President Donald Tresidder and Park Superintendent Washington B. Lewis stand in the alcove of the dining room. The Ahwahnee was carefully planned to ensure superb views of Glacier Point, Half Dome, and Yosemite Falls.

LEFT
From left to right, Interior Secretary Hubert Work, YP&CCo. President Donald Tresidder, NPS Director Stephen T. Mather, and YP&CCo. Vice President Robert T. Williams drive the stake for the proposed hotel on April 15, 1925.

ABOVE
While six-wheeled Fageol trucks hauled 680 tons of steel, 5,000 tons of stone, and 30,000 feet of timber to the building site and garnered the attention of the *Stockton Record* as "one of the most remarkable accomplishments in California automotive history," old-fashioned horsepower was often employed for construction.

The location of The Ahwahnee was similar in its context to that where Underwood's Zion Lodge had been quite recently built. Both spots were nestled close to rocky slopes that provided natural backdrops for the structures. In the case of The Ahwahnee, the hotel would be framed beneath the concentric overhangs of the Royal Arches. By situating it so close to the cliffs, its creators were hoping that the building would become part of the scene rather than a foreign object within it. It also

One of the most notable aspects of Underwood's design is the shape of the building. Viewed from above, the exterior walls form a stylized "Y," its three spokes emanating from a central core. The shape forms one-third of the perimeter of a hexagon, long recognized as one of the most efficient shapes in the natural world. The angle at which the

THE AHWAHNEE LANDSCAPE

served to make the massive structure seem smaller than it is, given the enormous scale of Yosemite's towering walls. Months were spent determining how to orient the hotel in order to preserve as many trees as possible, with an eye to screening the building while ensuring views from all the bedrooms and public areas.

In a memo to Fredrick Law Olmsted, Jr., regarding the landscape plans for the hotel, Donald Tresidder explained that "The Ahwahnee is located in such a way as to have superb views which embrace Glacier Point, Half Dome, Yosemite Falls, the Royal Arches. . . . It also offered a location ideally suited for Winter and Summer business because it afforded a maximum amount of available Winter sun and during the Summer had sufficient forests surrounding it to relieve the extreme heat of the north wall of the valley."

wings extend from the core takes advantage of the movement of the sun from one horizon to the other and permits the majority of guest rooms to have unimpeded views of the park's famous landmarks without providing direct views into other guest rooms. The public areas, with immense windows framing the beetling cliffs and picturesque forests, have even more spectacular views.

Underwood's innovatively-shaped hotel also allowed for a more compact design that conserved the surrounding landscape and provided greater visual interest to the building's exterior than a classic box design could ever have achieved.

The stair-stepped fashion by which the central core rises to a height of six stories mimics the irregular nature of the granite benches that serve as a backdrop for the hotel. The hip roofs reinforce a subtle triangular motif,

"It was desired from the beginning to make
The Ahwahnee environmental in its architecture,
rather than to follow any definite period."

—DONALD TRESIDDER

The stair-stepped design of the
hotel's southern façade mimics the
granite cliffs and benches that
serve as its backdrop.

ABOVE
By carefully considering the size and placement of the hotel's exterior stones, Underwood hoped to achieve a "rough and primitive appearance." To exaggerate the impression that the rock was piled naturally, he instructed that the stones be set "with the largest stone at the bottom gradually reducing the size of the stone being used at the upper finish."

BELOW
The hotel's siding, which appears to be redwood, is, in fact, concrete. The visual deception was achieved by pouring concrete into molds made of rough-sawn wood, then staining it the color of the surrounding pines.

the apex being the top of the building. From this top point, the mass of the structure spreads downward and outward like an alluvial fan. The three wings of the building echo this dynamic, extending from the core like massive tree roots. Even the stone columns, narrow at the top, flare outward at their bases. The effect is superb. A 1997 Historical Structures Report describes the result as "a kind of architectural rockpile given the tumble-down quality of its stone masonry."

Underwood clearly worked to emphasize this feeling, which is evident in his incorporation of more granite into the hotel's southern façade. By carefully combining the size and placement of the stones, he hoped to achieve a "rough and primitive appearance," reinforced with a sense of age accomplished by orienting the weathered surface of the stone outward. To exaggerate the

notion that the rock was piled naturally, he called for the stones to be set "with the largest stone at the bottom gradually reducing the size of the stone being used at the upper finish." A range of sizes "from four-man to two-man stones" was used, the size of the stone reflecting the number of men needed to hoist it.

As a result of Underwood's careful consideration, the hotel's granite columns and chimneys merge with the talus slope below Royal Arches when viewed from the south. Likewise, the eastern and western façades are made up of stone columns alternating with redwood-colored stained concrete, allowing the immense structure to mingle with the surrounding forest of black oak and ponderosa pine.

The real beauty in these efforts, however, is Underwood's ability to achieve a rustic appearance using modern materials. The hotel's exterior gives the impression of a structure composed of heavy timbers with wood siding, supported by massive stone columns. It is, however, primarily concrete and steel. Though not completely fireproof as originally planned, the structure is "fire resistant," and Underwood came close to achieving his original mandate.

The stone columns mask the steel and reinforced concrete skeleton of the hotel, which, although more expensive, was considered to be more durable than a simple reinforced concrete structure. The massive pine columns that support the truss ceiling of the dining room are actually hollow, cleverly disguising concrete-encased steel pillars that really do the work.

LEFT
When viewed from the talus slope to its north, the hotel is nearly invisible, its slate roof blending into the jumble of granite boulders that have tumbled down from Royal Arches over thousands of years.

The siding, which appears to be redwood, is concrete. The visual deception was again the result of careful planning; the concrete was poured into molds made of rough-sawn wood, then stained in the rich red color of the park's famous sequoias. In this manner, the concrete acquired the texture of the rough-sawn wood, and took on the look of a weathered plank. Window sills, balconies, and false beams jutting from the building's façade were all created in the same fashion.

One structure that is exactly what it appears to be is the wooden walkway that connects the porte cochère with the hotel's "entrance." Probably the last of the many changes that Under-wood made to the building's design, the walkway was hastily added to the hotel only ten days before its grand opening. The order to build it came after officials realized that the noise and exhaust from arriving vehicles would disturb guests staying in the rooms above the architect's originally-intended entrance (the present-day Ahwahnee Lounge).

RIGHT
Frederick Law Olmsted, Jr., recommended that a gate be constructed to give visitors approaching the hotel a sense of arrival. In 1930, jack-of-all-trades Bill Kat supervised construction of the unique stone gatehouse that now greets guests. Kat took great pride in the fact that the cantilevered stones were assembled without the use of any supporting understructure.

LEFT
The wooden walkway leading from the porte cochère to the hotel lobby was a last minute addition made after planners realized that noise and fumes from automobiles entering the original porte cochère (what is now the Ahwahnee Lounge) would disturb guests in the rooms above.

"The noble Redskin is now a blurred and pallid myth.
Hiawatha of sentimental romance, the pathetically melodi-
ous maidens of Indian love song and the valiant chiefs of
contraband dime novels have faded away. But in their
place has come a new respect for the real Indian, a recog-
nition of the Indian as an artist, as dancer, musician, story
teller, craftsman and above all, designer."

—DR. PHYLLIS ACKERMAN

POPE AND ACKERMAN

The hotel's exterior is unquestionably magnificent, but it is the public spaces of the interior that define The Ahwahnee and create the most lasting impressions. Here, Underwood's mastery of scale and texture is married with an innovative and sophisticated design scheme that seamlessly integrates elements from "twenty-two countries and districts on four continents" with the art of California's original inhabitants.

The Native American decorative theme and the hotel's name have been attributed to Donald and Mary Curry Tresidder, who shared an interest in the culture of Yosemite's indigenous peoples. But it would require a talented artist or artists to orchestrate the building's interior design. YP&CCo.'s search for a decorator began in May of 1926. No likely candidate could be indentifed, and Ansel Adams recounts in his autobiography that one of the directors "visited the completed structure and was appalled by the plans for the yet unfinished interior decoration. The main hall was to be furnished with black leather-covered sofas and buffalo heads were to be hung on the expansive walls."

The exasperated board member called on Albert Bender, a wealthy patron of the arts who published Adams's first portfolio, for advice. Bender suggested Dr. Arthur Upham Pope and Phyllis Ackerman, who were considered to be the foremost experts in Persian arts. By December, they were hired.

Dr. Arthur Upham Pope was a professor of philosophy at U.C. Berkeley when he met his bride-to-be, Dr. Phyllis Ackerman. A student in the School of Architecture, Ackerman shared Pope's electric intellect, tireless energy, and fascination with mid-Eastern art. They married in 1920, and according to a July, 1945 *New Yorker* article, were soon "acting for some of the wealthiest people in the country," purchasing rugs, tapestry, and pottery.

The pair had complete oversight of the decoration at The Ahwahnee, including choice of fabrics, rugs, paint, custom-made wrought iron lighting fixtures, and a wide variety of furniture, much of it custom crafted to their specifications. Demonstrating none of the indecision that seemed to plague the YP&CCo. board and challenge the architect, Pope and Ackerman approached their task with unwavering confidence.

Their assignment was to ensure that the atmosphere of the hotel "would be that of a quiet, luxurious country home." But Ackerman and Pope didn't settle for a simple approach such as distributing baskets and rugs throughout the rooms; they aspired to transform the impressive building into a work of art.

This rare color photograph by renowned photographer Ansel Adams (to document the hotel's condition in 1941) is one of a series that records The Ahwahnee's original décor. Besides capturing the fabrics and floor coverings, it also shows the beautiful color medallions that previously adorned the ceiling beams of the Great Lounge. Photograph by Ansel Adams, YP&CCo. Collection, courtesy of The Ansel Adams Publishing Rights Trust.

The floor of The Ahwahnee lobby features six inlaid mosaics designed by San Francisco artist, Henry Temple Howard. The colorful yet durable inlays are fabricated from battleship grade linoleum (a mixture of cork, saw dust, clay, and linseed oil that is cured under heat and compression). The geometric patterns are derived from California Native American basket designs, echoing the wrought iron and stenciled wall details.

The Fabric of Design

By associating it with universally acknowledged Mid-Eastern arts, the designers highlighted and elevated the work of Native Americans to unprecedented status. The geometric shapes became the foundation for their design plan, linking primitive cultures worldwide through the aesthetics of baskets, textiles, pottery, paintings, and beadwork. The treatment of the Indian designs showed their makers to have been "creative artists of ingenuity, sensitiveness and dignity."

To pull off this remarkable triumph, Ackerman and Pope turned to the Bay Area artistic community for assistance. There was little need to look beyond the U.C. Berkeley campus for talent. Indeed, most of the artists they engaged had ties to the university's School of Architecture.

the human relationship with nature. They combined ordinary media—textiles, glass, and paint—in extraordinary ways to bring life to the hotel's interior.

First Impressions

The art deco floor designs of the hotel lobby were prepared by artist and architect, Henry Temple Howard. Howard was later named the assistant architect of San Francisco's Coit Tower, and worked with former NPS architect Mark Daniels on the Ping Yuen Housing Project in Chinatown. For The Ahwahnee, he created six mosaics, each unique in color and geometry, that were inspired by patterns found on the baskets of the Yurok, Hupa, and Pomo tribes of California. Howard used a mix of black and brown hues most common to the baskets, but incorpo-

"If you want a golden rule that will fit, this is it: Have nothing in your houses that you do not know to be useful or believe to be beautiful." —WILLIAM MORRIS

The "megalithic" structure that Underwood had devised was a very masculine space. Some Yosemite Valley residents who observed the structure going up joked that Underwood was constructing a "Texas-sized railroad station" in Yosemite Valley. To contradict this impression, Ackerman and Pope worked hard to refine Underwood's general architectural statement by rounding the building's hard edges and personalizing the grand spaces. Softer, more feminine elements were introduced emphasizing color and texture and celebrating

rated objects such as red, yellow, and blue bird feathers to create his own brilliant palette.

Ringed with brass wire, the mosaics are often described as "rubber tile" though they are actually composed of battleship

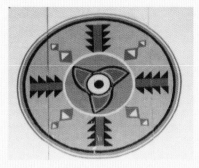

grade linoleum, a combination of cork, saw dust, clay, and linseed oil that is joined through heat and pressure. When installed in 1927, the mosaics "introduced a new method, both technically and artistically." A guest at The Ahwahnee once recounted that his father had assisted with the original installation. He claimed that since the process was not yet patented, tents were erected around the workers to shield the method from prying eyes.

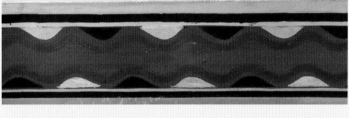

The lobby also establishes the use of room-banding stencils as a decorative element to link the various spaces. The stencils of The Ahwahnee are a diverse collection of individual designs with minimal repetition. Close to 100 different patterns were created to meet the needs of the lobby, lounge, and hallways. In addition, each guest room features a unique design above the door.

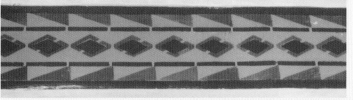

The lobby, separate from the main guest areas of the hotel, includes around its perimeter a gift shop, the front desk, the Sweet Shop, the concierge desk, and the Ahwahnee Lounge.

Originally an unwalled porte cochère, the Indian Room (now called the Ahwahnee Lounge) was Underwood's intended entrance to the hotel and, before the change, provided a much more dramatic first impression than the hastily-added side entrance walkway offers. From its perspective, the distant fireplace of the elevator lobby beckons with the promise of

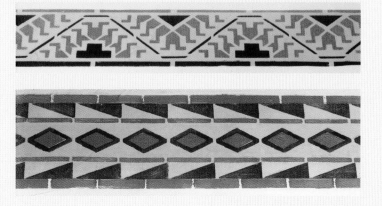

Jeannette Dyer Spencer created nearly a hundred unique stencil designs that adorn the walls, beams, and door frames of The Ahwahnee. The stencils tie together disparate components of the hotel. Spencer based her designs on patterns she found at the UC Berkeley library in books by Alfred Kroeber, at the time the foremost authority on the art and culture of California's indigenous people. Photographs by Charles Cramer, NPS Collection.

ABOVE
Rather than a building housing a collection of interesting artifacts, The Ahwahnee is a work of art. For example, over the fireplace in the elevator lobby, Jeanette Dyer Spencer painted her beautiful "basket-swirl-mural" directly onto the wall. For each guest room door, a unique design was stenciled above the transom.

BACKGROUND
A detail of the Great Lounge ceiling with chandeliers designed by Milton Roller of Phoenix Day Lighting in San Francisco. Photograph by N. Montanus, courtesy of Communications Department, DNC.

According to author George O'Bannon of *Oriental Rug Review*, the kelim display at The Ahwahnee includes the entire range of Middle Eastern flatweave techniques and is the only collection of its kind ever assembled by Persian art experts Arthur Upham Pope and Dr. Phyllis Ackerman.

more intimate and tranquil surroundings.

The entrance lobby and passage to the elevator lobby are lined with beautiful watercolors (not part of the hotel's original design scheme) depicting the park's memorable vistas. The paintings are by Gunnar Widforss, a Swedish-born artist whose work was popular with European royalty. Widforss fell in love with the vast landscapes of the American West, and after meeting with Stephen T. Mather in 1922, devoted himself to becoming "The Painter of the National Parks."

The elevator lobby, draped with some of the rare kelim carpets Pope and Ackerman purchased for the hotel, is a compact space and hub of activity with guests waiting for dinner or relaxing by the fire. Two sofas stand opposite each other in front of a large fireplace faced with native jasper, above which is one of the building's most distinctive artistic efforts. Jeanette Dyer Spencer, whose handiwork appears throughout The Ahwahnee, painted this stunning mural of overlapping basket patterns. By painting the wall instead of simply hanging a painting, the designers made the artwork integral to the hotel.

Underwood's biographer, Joyce Zaitlin, points out that the archi-

tect's decision to overscale the fireplace and the stonework of the stairway here, heightens the contrast between this room and those to come.

The chandeliers in the elevator lobby, like those in the entrance lobby, are modeled after those of the German Gothic period, but their detailing draws on Native American designs for inspiration, proving in Ackerman's words, "the admirable ease with which the California Indian motifs may be adapted." Milton Roller of Phoenix Day Lighting in San Francisco created these and the hotel's other distinctive wrought iron chandeliers.

Native American beadwork was the inspiration for the bold red and black geometric patterns that surround the elevator doors and service entrance flanking the stairway opposite the fireplace. When the hotel first opened, similar designs adorned the elevator doors themselves, and an elevator operator added a touch of class to the guest experience. A new guest elevator was installed in 1963, but the service elevator is original equipment.

Up the jasper-trimmed stairs are the mezzanine and what used to be the "women's lounge." Here sophisticated ladies could socialize, have their hair done, and dine in a private dining room overlooking the main dining room. The beauty parlor was relocated to the Village Store in 1959, while the private dining room became the El Dorado Diggins bar after prohibition, then was converted to a guest suite in the 1980s. Now only the women's restroom remains from the original second floor lounge.

Great Expectations

Guests stepping from the close confines of the elevator lobby into the Great Lounge almost universally announce their entrance into this marvelous space with an audible gasp. The room expands in all directions at once, rising up to cathedral-like dimensions.

In an effort to maintain a tranquil atmosphere in the lounge, acoustics experts were hired, and builders employed "practically every discovery to defeat the existence of disturbing sounds from both the outside and the inside." These included noise-proof plaster for all the interior walls and the elevator shafts, a special noiseless elevator, and heavily-padded floor coverings to assist in reducing sounds.

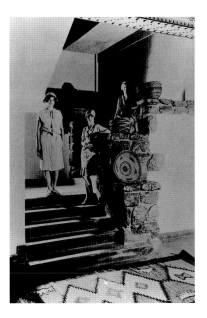

For art enthusiasts, it is no doubt startling to look back at historic images of the hotel and see rugs and baskets that any museum would prize, being used in a utilitarian fashion. Fortunately, many were encased for display purposes in the 1970s.

LEFT
Vernal Fall, an original watercolor by Gunnar Widforss that hangs in the lobby of The Ahwahnee. The paintings, intended for retail sale and promotion, were not part of the hotel's original design scheme. Widforss often exchanged his paintings for necessities, and in 1925 he signed a contract with Yosemite Park and Curry Co. whereby he traded paintings at two-thirds their normal prices for room and board. Photograph courtesy of DNC.

BELOW
A photographer captured a pair of women watching Gunnar Widforss paint at Bridalveil Fall. Widforss worked in oil, but it is his watercolors for which he is known best. His full-sheet paintings of Yosemite Falls, Vernal Fall, and the giant sequoias, among others, lend themselves beautifully to the scale of The Ahwahnee.

Gunnar Widforss

By the time Gunnar Widforss arrived in Yosemite in the 1920s, he was already famous among Europe's royalty for his beautifully expressive paintings. It was America's good fortune that he made the acquaintance of Stephen T. Mather, the tireless parks promoter and first director of the National Park Service. Widforss was traveling the world in search of compelling landscapes when Mather convinced him that the best to be found were in the American national parks.

A native of Stockholm, Sweden, Widforss was impish in stature and personality, a lighthearted soul who considered the great outdoors his studio. He studied to be a muralist at the Technical School at Stockholm from 1896 to 1900 and later at Academie Calcrossi in Paris. From age 29, he devoted himself fully to his art, traveling extensively in pursuit of subjects. He worked in oils and watercolors, but it is his images in the latter medium for which he is best known. His distinctive approach featured a subdued palette and a generally realistic style perfect for illustrating the atmospheric qualities of the immense vistas he painted.

So taken was he with the American landscape that Widforss obtained United States citizenship and opened a studio at his favorite location, the Grand Canyon, where he painted until his death in 1934. A collection of his original paintings hang in the lobby of The Ahwahnee, their muted colors and soft edges blending beautifully with the décor of the hotel.

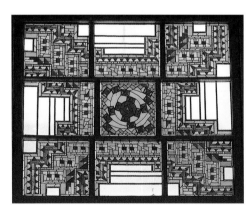

Officials "spent many hours try-ing to figure out some way to keep the noise from the roar of the Yosemite Falls out of the Hotel." Admitting defeat in an interview with the *Stockton Record*, the hotel's architect, Gilbert Stanley Underwood, observed, "even though we might attempt to eliminate the song of the falls, it is doubtful whether such could be arranged, even with the excellent standards of acoustical construc-tion to be found in The Ahwahnee."

Acoustics aside, the décor of the hotel contributes significantly to the building's tranquil mood. In the Great Lounge, ten immense multi-paned windows alternate with textured plaster columns to form the sides of the room. Crowning each is a five-foot-by-six-foot stained glass window, which adds to the room's cathe-dral-like personality.

Ackerman was greatly displeased with Underwood's original plan for the windows, describing the design as "execrable." She and Pope had on two occasions sub-mitted detailed drawings to Underwood suggesting a remedy that he chose to ignore. Out-

raged, Ackerman turned to Tresidder in March of 1927 for the authority to "put something in those frames that will take the curse off them."

The "something" was stained glass. The windows were to be of different patterns that, taken together, formed "a rhythmical frieze, banding the room." Acker-man and Pope selected Jeannette Dyer Spencer to carry out the task.

A graduate of U.C. Berkeley School of Architecture who had studied stained glass in Paris, Spencer approached her assign-ment with enthusiasm; she steeped herself in Native Ameri-can designs by pouring through books in the U.C. Berkeley Library by Alfred Kroeber, an authority on the art and culture of California's indigenous people. With machine-like efficiency, she designed and constructed the ten extraordinary windows in time for the hotel's July grand opening.

Ackerman was thoroughly satisfied with the results, stating that the windows represented "the renewal of vitality in a type of design which has, for some two hundred years, languished in arid artificiality." Upon completion of the entire project, Pope and Ackerman paid Spencer the ulti-mate compliment, recommending that Jeannette and her architect husband Ted be retained by YP&CCo. as architectural and design consultants, to ensure the continuity of the hotel's original atmosphere. The outcome was a professional relationship between YP&CCo. and the Spencers that lasted for nearly fifty years.

Jeannette Dyer Spencer is also responsible for the colorful stencils that appear throughout the hotel. In the Great Lounge, the decorated ceiling beams unite the various design elements, resulting in a room that is spacious, but not intimidating. The diversity of the design continually provides guests with opportunities to discover new facets of the hotel's décor.

When the hotel underwent renovation during the winter of 1996–97, oversize photographs depicting individuals from Yosemite's past were added to the walls of the Great Lounge, and many of the artifacts that were assembled by the Spencers to decorate the former El Dorado Diggins bar were taken out of storage and put on display on top of the six secretaries that line the walls. In addition, new wrought-iron light "trees" were commissioned for the large oak tables.

Underwood included a fireplace in nearly all of the public spaces, though the two at opposite ends of the Great Lounge are undoubtedly the most memorable. Scaled to match the dimensions of the room, these monumental sandstone hearths are surprisingly efficient. Both are tall enough for an adult to stand in, and each features a pair of built-in benches.

A Change of Pace

Beyond the Great Lounge the public spaces adopt a different feeling, though in some cases they still retain a fingerhold on the hotel design theme through fabric choices, framed rug fragments, and Gothic chandeliers. Pope and Ackerman intended these rooms to provide a sense of contrast and relief from the Native American elements.

ABOVE
After the Navy vacated The Ahwahnee following World War II, Frann Spencer Reynolds (daughter of Jeannette Dyer Spencer) was commissioned to create a new Mondrian-style mural on the north wall of the Great Lounge above the fireplace. The mural remained until the early 1980s, when the original 1927 appearance was restored (without the medallions on the ceiling beams). Photograph courtesy of DNC.

TOP
Most of the chairs, sofas, and tables in the Great Lounge today were in use when the hotel opened in 1927, though they do sport new fabrics and upholstery.

Vintage photographs by Ansel Adams and David Brower in the Winter Club Room (originally known as the California Room) depict club members engaged in an array of winter activities. Many of the images showcase the exquisite natural beauty of Yosemite Valley. The Yosemite Winter Club, chartered in 1928 to promote winter sports, was headquartered in this room for many years.

The quiet trickle of the jasper fountain in the spacious, sun-drenched solarium is a captivating sound. Dr. Phyllis Ackerman, one of the hotel's original decorators, noted that the room and its five floor-to-ceiling windows achieve "the pleasant sense of being merely a sheltered bit of outdoors."

To the southeast is the California Room, originally decorated to commemorate the days of the Gold Rush with miner's lamp chandeliers, checked curtains, and animal skins. Eventually, the room became the headquarters for the Yosemite Winter Club, and the symbols of "frontier luxury"—a polar bear rug and a buffalo robe—were replaced with trophy cases and walls of black and white photographs depicting winter activities. Represented photographers include Ansel Adams and David Brower, both of whom did publicity work for YP&CCo.

In the crescent-shaped Solarium, the ceiling soars skyward once again to accommodate five, two-story-high windows. This is a classic Underwood design motif. He had a fondness for framing the landscape with immense pieces of glass, and repeated the concept in his designs for the inn on the North Rim of the Grand Canyon and for Jackson Lake Lodge in the Tetons. At the time, windows of such proportions were rare even in cities, and much was made of the difficulty in safely transporting the heroic panes to such a remote location.

The interior design of the Solarium is understated. A jasper fountain gurgles quietly, its watery whisper typically the only sound emanating from this light-filled space, which Ackerman described as a "sheltered box seat for the out of doors." The sunny atmosphere and natural elegance of the room makes it a favorite place for weddings.

With the Great Lounge, the Writing or Mural Room is the only public space that features an oak floor. The floor complements the Colonial-style chandelier, dark paneled walls, low slung chairs, and a unique hammered-copper corner fireplace. The focal point of the space remains the *toile peinte*, or painted linen, in beautiful fifteenth-century style. Artist Robert Boardman Howard painted the mural in the *mille fleurs* tradition, creating a pattern of flowering plants interspersed with the local wildlife; the piece is not only decorative, but also serves as an illustrated nature guide for the park.

A stairway ascends from the Solarium to a set of balconied meeting rooms. The Tudor Lounge, the largest and central room, overlooks the Great Lounge and mirrors the mezzanine above the Elevator Lobby. Flanking it on either side are the Colonial and Tresidder Rooms, each equipped with a fireplace, colonial Williamsburg-style chandeliers, and a pair of outdoor balconies. The Tudor Lounge has long served as the location for the presentation of interpretive films. The Tresidder Room was originally known as the Game Room, and for many years was devoted to ping pong.

Décor is noticeably subdued in these rooms, though the walls are brightened by a substantial collection of contemporary Yosemite artwork and photography. Beginning in the mid-1980s, works were selected from the award-winners of the Yosemite Renaissance, an annual park-based art competition. Many of the pieces were created by park artists, including Jane Gyer, Linda Abbott, Sally Owens, and Dudley Kendall.

A Feast for the Senses

Stripped of all décor, the Dining Room would remain the most impressive space in The Ahwahnee. The dimensions alone are improbable, and the emotional impact is immeasurable. The room was Underwood's most emphatic statement in The Ahwahnee's public areas.

At 130 feet long and 51 feet wide, this is the largest room in the hotel. Its 34-foot-high vaulted ceiling is striped with peeled log trusses held aloft by massive stone and sugar pine columns alternating with eleven 24-foot-high plate glass windows. Adding to the amazing ambience are tangy aromas, translucent light, piano music, and conviviality. The Ahwahnee Dining Room is not so much a dinner hall as it is an experience.

Given this leviathan scale, it's hard to believe that original plans called for a room nearly three times its present size. Even as the

ABOVE
Dr. Phyllis Ackerman wanted the décor of the Mural Room (also called the Writing Room), with its hammered copper fireplace, dark wood paneling, and mural, to provide contrast and relief from the rest of the building's Native American theme.

SIDEBAR DETAILS
The *toile peinte* (painted tapestry) of the Mural Room is typical of those found in Northern Europe in the fifteenth century. The painting by Robert Boardman Howard depicting the park's native flora and fauna is a wonderful decoration and illustrated nature guide.

cornerstone for the building was set in place, publicity materials were advertising "ample accommodations for 1,000 diners." Shortly thereafter, however, the space was scaled down to seat today's more "modest" maximum of 350 diners.

At the same time, another change was contemplated. A flat roof was proposed for the dining room, so that an outdoor dance pavilion

Robert Boardman Howard: An Artistic Contribution

Artist Robert Boardman Howard made significant contributions to The Ahwahnee and in Yosemite generally. His most notable work in the hotel is the *toile pente* he created for the Mural Room that still hangs there.

One of five talented children (his father, John Galen Howard, was the founder of the U.C. Berkeley School of Architecture), Robert Boardman Howard struggled in school as a youth, so his father removed him and arranged for Arthur Upham Pope to serve as his tutor. During World War I, Robert traveled to Europe with the Army. He was discharged shortly after arriving, so he packed his watercolors and rode his bicycle through the Netherlands, Belgium, France, Italy, and Greece, painting as he went. Occasionally, his brother Henry, who was studying architecture at the École des Beaux Arts, would join him.

After installing the mural he painted for The Ahwahnee in 1927, Robert joined fellow artists Chiura Obata and Worth Ryder on a six week camping trip in Yosemite's high country. Obata, who later joined the art faculty at U.C. Berkeley, produced over 150 watercolors on that trip, many of which are featured in the book *Obata's Yosemite*.

Howard also produced the "Calderesque" mobile for the Indian Room (now the Ahwahnee Lounge), and for the Badger Pass ski lodge several bas-relief fireplace panels, which have since been moved to the Mountain Room Lounge at Yosemite Lodge. His brother, Henry Temple Howard, created the six inlaid mosaics for the floor of The Ahwahnee lobby.

could be developed. Fortunately, the idea was rejected, and the airy expanse of pine timbers survived to add elegance to the ultimate Yosemite dining experience.

Like the Solarium, the room was so successful on its own that Pope and Ackerman did little to enhance it. A half dozen kelims hanging from the north wall, a few prominent stencils on the gables, and smaller, more numerous geometric figures painted along the roof line serve as ties to the hotel's Native American design theme. Additional geometric patterns are etched in the stained concrete floor, though they are mostly hidden beneath the tables.

A meal taken in these confines is the quintessential dining experience, for this is a place to linger and savor the grandeur of Yosemite. The windows provide views of the valley's awesome scale, unimpeded from top to bottom, with the most memorable vista afforded by the alcove at the far end of the room with its framed view of Upper Yosemite Fall.

Very little has changed since the first diners broke bread in this hallowed hall in 1927. The tables and chairs are original (cushions were added to the seats in recent years), and the silverware and china are the same patterns originated by Jeanette Dyer Spencer. The stately three-legged wrought iron candlesticks are hand-crafted using the same techniques employed in 1927. Chopin and Mozart still rise from the Steinway grand piano, and through the immense windows, one can still follow the gentle descent of a snowflake from cottony clouds high above.

"Dining is and always was a great artistic opportunity."

—FRANK LLOYD WRIGHT

The Ahwahnee dining room has been described as the most beautiful in any national park. Massive stone pillars and peeled sugar pine columns (with steel I-beam cores) alternate with immense windows and support a spectacular roof nearly half a football field in length. Even when the dining room is filled to capacity, its massive stone columns, immense picture windows, and 34-foot-high ceiling combine to create an uncrowded atmosphere.

WINTER TRADITIONS

The Ahwahnee was the first year-round hotel in Yosemite when it opened in 1927. But it would be many years before it hosted guests all year round. To help bolster business in the slack months, managers have created events and activities that provide potential guests with even greater incentives to choose Yosemite as their destination.

The Yosemite Winter Club—headquartered in The Ahwahnee for many years—was chartered in 1928 to promote winter sports. While both Donald and Mary Curry Tresidder were ski enthusiasts, minutes of the YP&CCo. board show that the company's commitment to the concept was not a passing fancy. Prominent persons throughout the state were asked to serve as honorary Winter Club officers, and members of the public were invited to become members for a small annual fee. In his role as YP&CCo. President, Tresidder was authorized to take whatever action was necessary to make the club effective, and the company agreed to be responsible for any deficit resulting from the club's activities.

Vintage photographs in the Winter Club Room (originally known as the California Room) depict members, with Yosemite Valley's stunning winter scene as a backdrop, engaged in an array of winter activities, including hockey tournaments, Olympic speed skating trials, downhill ski races, dogsledding, ski joring behind horses, and tobogganing on an enormous man-made run.

The first "ski hill" was established on the glacial moraine opposite the stables in 1928. A year later, a 60,000-square-foot ice rink was created by flooding the Curry Village parking lot. With this development, former U.S. President Herbert Hoover consented to sponsor a cup to be a permanent emblem of the Pacific Coast Championship in intercollegiate winter sports (to be hosted annually in Yosemite National Park).

Yosemite came very close to being the site of the winter Olympics in 1932 on the strength of its burgeoning winter programs. The narrow loss of the games to Lake Placid was disappointing at the time, but most now agree that it was a fortuitous outcome. The developmental pressure and related impacts of hosting the games would likely have changed the nature of the Yosemite experience.

In spite of the setback, winter business continued to "snowball." The first downhill ski area on the West Coast opened at Badger Pass in 1935. Two years later, The Ahwahnee began hosting a weekly "ski buffet" where guests could dine with the ski school's energetic instructors, and started a tradition that lasted for over fifty years. Dancing on the hotel's mezzanine (management was still struggling to find a suitable indoor location at the hotel) was contemplated but dismissed when it was determined that the building was not engineered to support the associated loads.

ABOVE
The dining room, beautiful any time of year, is the focal point for gala banquets during the Vintners' Holidays and Chefs' Holidays in autumn and winter respectively.

PREVIOUS PAGE
In winter, the rising sun warms The Ahwahnee's exterior, while in spring, the splashing of Royal Arch Cascade and the distant roar of Yosemite Falls fill the air. Come summer, the black oaks, majestic pines, maples, and dogwoods provide shade and seclusion, then enliven the hotel grounds with fall color.

Beginning in the early 1980s, a series of special events was organized at the hotel featuring photography, music, fine food, and wine. Of the four concepts, the "Chefs' Holiday" and "Vintners' Holiday" proved to have the broadest appeal, and became established as new traditions at The Ahwahnee.

neophytes, all of whom share a passion for both wine and Yosemite. Lectures and panel discussions by the winemakers mix humor, lively debate, and serious exploration of the wine industry, and are moderated by wine experts such as Master Sommelier Evan Goldstein and syndicated wine columnist Dan Berger.

ABOVE
Roland Henin (left), a former instructor at the Culinary Institute of America and coach of the United States team in the Culinary Olympics, demonstrates how to filet a salmon in The Ahwahnee's 6,500-square-foot kitchen. Hired to help improve food service parkwide, Henin is one of a handful of Certified Master Chefs in the United States and the first ever to receive the CIA's Chef of the Year award.

NEAR RIGHT
When The Ahwahnee was built in 1927, ice was used for refrigeration. The doors visible high above the three walk-in refrigerators were used to load the ice blocks. Inside, a roof-shaped hood above the food caught the meltwater and channeled it into a drain, while the heavier, cool air filled the space below.

FAR RIGHT
Ahwahnee pastry chef Ann Creswell stirs batter in a copper pot dating to the 1927 opening of The Ahwahnee. Most of the equipment in the kitchen has been upgraded through the years, but a few original pieces remain, functioning as well today as they did over seventy-five years ago.

A Celebration of Food and Wine

A successful event for over twenty seasons, the Vintners' Holiday annually gathers the cream of California's exceptionally-gifted pool of winemakers each fall in the Great Lounge of The Ahwahnee for a series of midweek seminars and tastings. Typically kicking off during the second week of November and continuing for a month, the wine events feature vintners from such wineries as Ferrari-Carano, Kenwood, Silver Oak, and Au Bon Climat, who share the stage with up-and-coming winemakers.

To accommodate the crowds of oenophiles, furniture in the Great Lounge is moved aside and rows of tables are set up, transforming the space into a "Great Classroom." Attendees range from lifelong wine enthusiasts to complete

But the lectures and tastings are only the beginning. Each two- and three-day session features four renowned vintners, and culminates in a "Gala Vintners' Dinner" in the majestic Ahwahnee dining room. This memorable banquet provides an opportunity for The Ahwahnee's executive chef and the guest winemakers to collaborate, as they marry extraordinary wines with a five-course gourmet meal.

Baker Craig Chase bakes homemade sourdough bread daily using a 150-year-old sourdough starter.

Chefs' Holidays

In January and February, culinary masters converge from all corners of the country at The Ahwahnee. Nationally-renowned chefs, such as Hubert Keller, Ken Frank, and Mark Hill, headline, as do legendary specialists such as Gayle Ortiz of Gayle's Bakery and Rotisserie and Bruce Aidell of Aidell's Sausage.

Sundays through Thursdays for four midwinter weeks the public areas of the hotel are filled with remarkable aromas as culinary enthusiasts seek to improve their skills. Once again, the Great Lounge is set up classroom style, with all the culinary essentials arranged on the dais for live cooking demonstrations. An immense mirror hovers above this portable kitchen ensuring that each and every move of the guest chefs is visible to the transfixed audience.

After sharing their secrets, the talented chefs for each session move into the 6,500-square-foot Ahwahnee kitchen to team up with the hotel's staff to prepare an extravagant five-course banquet that is served in the unparalleled atmosphere of the dining room.

Both the Vintners' and Chefs' Holidays are designed to permit guests to interact personally with the talented presenters, take in the demonstrations, and still have an opportunity for recreation and quiet contemplation in the park.

ABOVE
The Great Lounge is the scene of the annual Vintners' Holidays.

LEFT
Pastry Chef Ann Creswell works with a local florist to decorate a wedding cake in The Ahwahnee's pastry shop. When the hotel architect shrank the capacity of the dining room from 1,000 to 350 diners, the kitchen remained the same size. Hence, it is ideally suited to provide for special events in addition to normal food service. The hotel hosts an average of 175 weddings each year.

The Bracebridge Dinner, based on an 1819 story by Washington Irving, dramatizes a banquet in the manor of Squire Bracebridge of Yorkshire, England. A moving celebration of spirit, song, and fine food, the popular dinner has been staged nearly every Christmas since 1927.

The aromas of fresh pine, perfume, and wood smoke mingle in the air above a mixture of expectant conversation and Yuletide song in The Ahwahnee's Great Lounge. Abrubtly, a fanfare of trumpets silences the clamor as it summons the revelers to what is perhaps the nation's most famous Christmas dinner.

The doors of the The Ahwahnee dining room swing wide, and the hushed crowd enters the majestic, candlelit chamber. Women wearing gowns sparkling with gems and men outfitted in tights and feathered caps popular in the Renaissance greet the guests and escort them to their seats.

As a gong chimes rhythmically, the lights dim and a costumed procession of choristers enters the

"The Legend of Sleepy Hollow") penned in 1819 by Washington Irving under the name Geoffrey Crayon, Gent.

In Irving's classic story, Squire Bracebridge laments the loss of the tradition of making merry on Christmas and devotes himself to the preservation of old English hospitality: "I love," said he, "to see this day well kept by rich and poor; it is a great thing to have one day in the year, at least, when you are sure of being welcome wherever you go, and of having, as it were, the world all thrown open to you." The event's director, Andrea Fulton, believes that "The Bracebridge represents a Christmas that never was, but a Christmas that lives in everyone's hearts."

Now Christmas is come
Let us beat up the drum,
And call all our neighbours together;
And when they appear,
Let us make them such cheer,
As will keep out the wind and the weather.
—OLD ENGLISH SONG

The housekeeper announces "A noble feast awaits thee, Lord, The best my larder doth afford!" The Squire responds, "Thank thee, 'tis well! Be seated all! I bid ye hail to Bracebridge Hall!" The first Squire Bracebridge was played by Donald Tresidder, the first president of Yosemite Park and Curry Company. Since his death in 1948, the role has been played by individuals from the Stanford University theatre department.

THE BRACEBRIDGE DINNER

room solemnly singing "Let All Mortal Flesh Keep Silence." With faces illumined only by the slender candles they hold, the singers glide down the aisle. The barely-visible expressions of the guests reveal a blend of awe, delight, and surprise. And so begins another Bracebridge Dinner.

For the next three hours, occupants of this stately room will be transported back in time to old England, to be part of a Yosemite tradition that has continued nearly annually at The Ahwahnee since 1927. The 350 or so in attendance will be the pampered guests of the jovial Squire Bracebridge, a magnanimous character brought to life from the pages of *Old Christmas*, a heartwarming yarn out of the collection of stories in *The Sketchbook* (which includes "Rip Van Winkle" and

Music for the first Bracebridge Dinner was provided by an all-male chorus from San Francisco's celebrated Bohemian Club wearing powdered wigs.

The core dramatic elements of the Bracebridge Dinner have remained consistent since its inception, but the cast of characters and details of the performance change from year to year.

A Cause for Celebration

With the opening of The Ahwahnee, Yosemite Park & Curry Company president Donald Tresidder hoped to develop a Yosemite holiday pageant to entice guests to enjoy the park's winter splendor, while extending the company's business (typically at capacity in the summer) into the "off" season. He approached Garnett Holme, another creative talent with U.C. Berkeley connections, for help. Holme was the official National Park Service Pageant Master with an office in Yosemite and a bundle of pageants to his credit.

Only a year before, Holme had produced a pageant to help celebrate the 75th anniversary of the European discovery of Yosemite, performed the same weekend that the cornerstone of the hotel was ceremoniously placed. Taking note of the dining room's attributes, Holme suggested to Tresidder that no better model existed for the atmosphere that he sought to create at The Ahwahnee than Irving's imaginary Bracebridge Hall.

Holme developed a loose script combining drama, traditional music, and a meal, based fairly closely on the story. He cast the YP&CCo. president as Squire Bracebridge, a role Tresidder would play for the rest of his life with an enthusiasm that would have pleased Irving. A historic photo of one of the first dinners shows Tressider seated at the head table with his wife Mary, his mother-in-law Jennie Curry, his sister Oliene, and others, all adorned with powdered wigs favored by the eighteenth-century English gentry.

The Ahwahnee's first "Bracebridge" dinner based on *The Sketchbook* occurred on Christmas Day in 1927. Music was provided by an all-male chorus from San Francisco's celebrated Bohemian Club. Ansel Adams, who participated in the 1928 dinner, recalls in his autobiography that it was a "spirited" affair, in large part due to a pre-performance party at the singers' cabin, where bourbon and water, chilled by icicles from the cabin's shingled roof, flowed freely. The chorus members entered the dining room "in a state of convivial bliss."

A Change in Direction

When Garnett Holme died the following year, Adams was given the opportunity to apply his talents to the pageant. Tresidder invited Adams and Jeannette Dyer Spencer to take over the production. They agreed, inaugurating a partnership that endured for over forty years. Adams created promotional photographs, arranged the music, and oversaw the choir, while Spencer concentrated on costumes and decoration. Together they developed the grandeur and splendor for which the pageant is known today.

While Holme used a loose style, Adams gave the pageant a definite structure. He wrote the characters' lines in a rhymed, four-beat cadence, and searched out appropriately fine music (including "Green Groweth the Holly"—attributed to Henry the Eighth—and "The Coventry Carol"), while "avoiding the soupy and the banal." Another of his selections, "Cantique de Noel" ("O Holy Night"), performed by male and female soloists, now represents the essence of Bracebridge for many guests.

Minstrels, magicians, and other merry makers entertain Bracebridge guests between courses.

Looking back on his involvement with the event just a year prior to his death, Ansel Adams wrote, "I feel a certain pride about the Bracebridge; its aesthetics and style directly relate to the emotional potential of the natural scene. In Yosemite there is that certain grandeur and beauty which fine art and music enhance and inferior human endeavors denigrate."

Decorating Bracebridge Hall

Jeannette Dyer Spencer had earlier been responsible for the permanent decoration of The Ahwahnee dining room. She relished the freedom she was given to develop the props and costumes needed to duplicate the atmosphere of the great oaken hall on the fictional squire's rambling estate in Yorkshire, England.

She changed the costume style from eighteenth-century English to a mix of Renaissance and Medieval to reflect that described in Irving's humorous post-dinner procession. In the early years of the event, costumes were provided for guests as well as performers. The price of the dinner included a costume rental fee, and guests were encouraged to outfit themselves from a rack of options on the mezzanine.

Following her specifications, Jeanette's architect/husband Ted Spencer constructed an accurate representation of the hall's sideboard, which debuted as the backdrop to the head table in 1928. In a nod to whimsy, Jeanette added two wooden dogs to patiently sit by the table, intent on begging the squire for scraps each year.

But it was with stained glass that Jeanette Spencer left her mark on "Bracebridge Hall." She made the focal point of the room the alcove where a dais draped in valuable kelims supports the head table and sideboard. Banners reach out from the columns lining both walls and frame the glorious scene. Filling the immense space above is a magnificent, glowing stained-glass-style interpretation of the Madonna and Christ child attended by four angels offering incense, while shepherds gaze in adoration.

Atop the windows lining the room are faux glass rondels (circles) wreathed in holiday greens, each depicting a scene or one of the character's from Irving's tale. The brilliant colors of the stunning backdrop and the rondels were created with enamel on parchment, backlit to resemble the stained glass of medieval French cathedrals.

Changing of the Guard

Ansel Adams and Jeannette Dyer Spencer collaborated until World War II, when The Ahwahnee was closed to the public and converted to a Naval convalescent hospital. When the war ended, the Bracebridge tradition resumed, though with a number of changes. In 1946, YP&CCo. officials, uncertain whether the hotel would reopen in time for Christmas, waited until November before committing to a performance. Adams realized that the short notice and his burgeoning photography career wouldn't allow him the necessary time to direct the pageant on his own, so he enlisted Eugene Fulton, a talented choral conductor and voice teacher, as Musical Director.

Known for a keen wit as well as his photographic and musical skills, Ansel Adams played the Lord of Misrule for the first Bracebridge Dinner in 1927. Adams took over directing the Bracebridge Dinner after its originator, Garnett Holme, died.

Atop each of the windows lining the room is a faux glass rondel wreathed in holiday greens and depicting a scene from Irving's tale or from The Ahwahnee pageant's cast of characters. The brilliant colors of the stunning backdrop and the rondels are actually enamel on parchment, backlit to resemble glass of the medieval cathedrals Jeannette Dyer Spencer studied while at the École des Louvre.

In *The Bracebridge Dinner*, the 1953 publication she co-authored with Ansel Adams, Jeannette details her inspiration. "Two [rondels] show the Morris dancers the Squire welcomed to the Hall Christmas morning. Maid Marian and Tom Fool crowned with a foxskin dance gaily in one. In the others, two knights, Saint George and the Black Prince of Paladine, battle lustily. A third rondel depicts the trained bear and the hobby horse who in bygone times shared in the village revelries."

Two years later, Donald Tresidder's unexpected death presented a troubling dilemma. Some felt that YP&CCo.'s president had so thoroughly epitomized Squire Bracebridge, that it wouldn't be appropriate for anyone else to play the part. Rational thought won out over emotions, though, and a decision was made that the Squire, his Lady, and the Parson would be played by members of the Stanford University Theatre Department each year.

So it is that the warm and generous face of Stanford's George Willey became that of Squire Bracebridge for so many attendees. Before his death, Willey and his wife Jill played the parts of the Squire and his Lady for thirty-five years. Like many of the performers, they celebrated Christmas with their family each year by being part of the pageant, watching their children grow into and out of the costumes for villagers, wards, and servants.

The Eugene Fulton family probably has the most extensive association with the Bracebridge Dinner. Beginning in 1946, Fulton dedicated every single Christmas to refining the pageant until his death (following a dress rehearsal) at the hotel in 1979. His wife Anna-Marie, the organist and behind-the-scenes organizer for many years, and their daughter Andrea, whose career began as a five-year-old playing the part of a villager, rallied the stunned cast, which managed to complete the three dinners and a post-Christmas concert. Soon thereafter, Andrea was passed the mantle of director.

Musically sophisticated and intimately familiar with the origins of the traditions acted out in the Bracebridge, Andrea Fulton scripted the opening poem, wrote the "Villagers Song," and added English translations to many of the choral pieces. Each year, using the original framework of the dinner as a foundation, she has introduced additional characters and subtle changes. One such change is an increase in the number and prominence of female vocalists. The additional female voices have given the dinner a greater sense of lightness, hope, and brightness.

Food for the Soul

The "dinner" portion of Bracebridge is a seven-course extravaganza combining drama, symbolism, and fine food. The sounding of a gong announces each course, and the chorus parades up the main aisle escorting lackeys bearing an oversize representation of the upcoming fare. When they reach the head table the Squire passes judgment on the proffered dish. Between the elaborate presentations, the "Lord of Misrule" makes a humorous nuisance of himself, minstrels wander, and the chorale continues its enchanting performance.

The actual menu changes from year to year, but the order and substance of the four main courses—fish, poultry, beef, and pudding—have remained essentially unchanged since the first dinner. It is the Parson's duty to "preach the fare." Climbing to the pulpit before the arrival of each menu item, he recites verse Ansel Adams authored in 1929.

First on the list is the fish, a symbol of Christianity.

"There comes, I see, a seemly dish — Indeed, no other than the Fish!"

Once the fish (and each subsequent dish) is approved by the Squire, a parade of waiters and waitresses streams forth to serve the entire hall within minutes. Though "officially" discouraged, the diners often respond to the arrival of their server with competing rounds of applause.

In the midst of enjoying the first course, diners along the windows of the hall find themselves gazing into the mournful eyes of a tattered band of adults and children peering in from the chilly out-of-doors. These "villagers" have traditionally been played by employees and residents of Yosemite Valley.

The second course, Peacock Pie, is carried in with pomp, its "feathers spread, and head held high." According to Irving, "Such pies were served up at the solemn banquets of chivalry, when Knights-errant pledged themselves to undertake any perilous enterprise." While peacock was historically used for the dish, in modern times, pheasant or quail is often substituted.

The Boar's Head and Baron of Beef, carried on separate litters, are the next to arrive. Symbolic of many beliefs, the Boar's Head is presented to the Squire, who announces with a wave of his hand,

"The bravest dish in all the land! Honored of old, I understand — Needless to dwell upon thy fame!"

Members of the Bracebridge cast stand at the head table awaiting the entrance of Squire Bracebridge.

Mrs. Ollo Baldauf played the minstrel in this early Bracebridge Dinner. A variation of this photograph by Ansel Adams appeared on the cover of *Life Magazine* in December, 1938. Photograph by Ansel Adams, courtesy of the Yosemite Research Library.

Then offered the beef platter, he takes an immense carving knife from the chef and with a ceremonial flourish continues,

"Another dish of ancient name,
Deserves high rank!
With gesture brief I knight
thee, Sir Loin,
Baron of Beef!"

The final course of the dinner, the Wassail and Plum Pudding, is announced by the Parson with great enthusiasm.

"Rich in every luscious detail
Comes the Pudding and the Wassail!
Merry men with buoyant song
Bear the final course along!"

To which the Jester exclaims,

"Zounds! At last the Wassail goes the rounds!"

In Irving's tale, the Squire mixed the wassail himself, using the "richest and raciest wines, highly spiced and sweetened with roasted apples," and called its bowl "the ancient fountain of good feeling, where all hearts met together." The Bracebridge Dinner's wassail has a wonderful, traditional flavor without an intoxicating effect, though by the end of this memorable meal, one would guess it was the authentic item.

Encore!

In 1956, the popularity of the Bracebridge necessitated an additional Christmas Day performance. A lottery was instituted in 1977 to ensure egalitarian distribution of the prized tickets, and just a year later, a third performance was scheduled for Christmas Eve. Two more performances were added for December 22 in

the mid-1980s. The lottery was abandoned after some twenty-five years, and the squire now bids "Ye welcome to Bracebridge Hall" eight times each year; dinners are scheduled December 15, 16, 18, 19, 21, 22, Christmas Eve, and Christmas Day.

A few of the seats are offered to guests for whom Bracebridge has been a family tradition since long before the lottery was in place. Beginning in 1977, seats at the head table have been provided to selected couples, who serve as the Visiting Squire and Lady. The list of fortunates who have donned tights and cockaded hats includes locals, National Park Service brass, dignitaries such as the Governor of California, and Ansel and Virginia Adams in 1979.

All told, over 100 singers and dining room employees join forces to entertain and serve 350 guests at each seating. In the kitchen, another 100 toil away in anonymity, their machine-like movements guaranteeing efficient delivery of the memorable meal.

What undoubtedly makes the Bracebridge Dinner so popular with guests is the authenticity of the warm feelings and joy that surround this annual celebration. Washington Irving wrote, "Surely happiness is reflective, like the light of heaven; and every countenance, bright with smiles, and glowing with innocent enjoyment, is a mirror transmitting to others the rays of a supreme and ever-shining benevolence."

CELEBRITY GUESTS

Actress Kim Novak brought her own purple sheets. President John F. Kennedy imported his orthopedic bed. Ethiopian Emperor Haile Selassie was accompanied by a staff of eighteen and half a ton of luggage, including his favorite elephant tusks. Prince Philip outdid them all as escort for the Queen of England, with an entourage of forty-two in tow. Over the years The Ahwahnee has served as home away from home for the noble, the famous, and the well-heeled, hosting royalty, stage and screen stars, politicians, authors, and athletes alike.

Queen Elizabeth's visit in March of 1983 was the most widely reported, but hers was not the first royal visit. Emperor Selassie visited in 1954, King Baudouin of Belgium came in 1959, and Queen Ratana of Nepal and the exiled Shah of Iran, Mohammed Rezi Pahlavi, both roomed at The Ahwahnee in 1960.

Four presidents of the United States have stayed at The Ahwahnee, but only John F. Kennedy did so while he was in office. Kennedy flew into Yosemite Valley in a helicopter in August of 1962. He spent just one night in the hotel, but his peak-season visit made a big splash. His own orthopedic bed was moved into what is now known as the "Presidential Suite," and the occupants of the entire second and third floors of the hotel were moved out during his stay for security reasons.

When Kennedy requested fresh trout for dinner, fly fishermen were dispatched to catch some. The president was still enjoying his trout when the Firefall, normally scheduled at precisely 9 P.M., was set to be staged. Anxiety built as the entertainers at Camp Curry did their best to stall the waiting crowd until the president was ready. Extra red fir bark was gathered earlier in the day, so when the handlers finally pushed the glowing coals off the face of Glacier Point, the display was more spectacular than ever.

First Lady Laura Bush spent one night at The Ahwahnee in 2001 after hiking to several High Sierra Camps with friends and a retinue of secret service agents. The hotel's executive chef, Robert Anderson, was called upon to prepare dinner for the entourage. He says that being summoned to the First Lady's room where she told him how much she enjoyed the meal he had prepared was the highlight of his career. First Lady Eleanor Roosevelt, for whom Yosemite's Roosevelt Lake is named, also enjoyed The Ahwahnee, but preferred the park's rugged backcountry.

If he were alive today, Stephen T. Mather would be proud. This parade of celebrities through his "luxury hotel" was precisely what he had hoped for. He believed that with each dignitary's visit, Yosemite and the entire national park system would gain an influential and enthusiastic fan.

Lucille Ball on the set of *The Long, Long Trailer* in 1947. The film is one of many that use Yosemite as a backdrop. Photograph courtesy of DNC.

ABOVE
Robert Francis portrayed Ensign Willie Keith and May Wynn appeared as his girlfriend vacationing at The Ahwahnee in the classic war drama, *The Caine Mutiny*. Photograph courtesy of Sony Pictures.

BELOW
President John F. Kennedy in the hotel elevator with Bob Maynard, the manager of The Ahwahnee at the time. Four U.S. presidents have stayed at the hotel, but only Kennedy did so while in office. Photograph courtesy of Nancy Maynard.

He might have had second thoughts about his plan, however, after the first group of V.I.P.s attended a complimentary, pre-opening party in 1927.

About fifty guests, including the YP&CCo. board of directors and their wives, attended an invitation-only affair the evening before the hotel officially opened to the public, according to historian Shirley Sargent. They departed the following morning with more than memories. The special guests pocketed everything from pewter ink stands to hand-loomed blankets and bedspreads; they even walked off with some of the valuable baskets that had been on display. This was certainly not the behavior that Mather might have expected from guests at a hotel with its own English butler!

Lucille Ball, Desi Arnaz, and Judy Garland were chastised as well in 1947 for conducting a late night concert on the Steinway in the Great Lounge while they were in the park for the filming of the comedy, *The Long, Long Trailer*. Though miffed at the time, Lucy and Desi returned in 1955 while making *Forever Darling*.

The Ahwahnee was used as a set in the film *The Caine Mutiny*, which starred Humphrey Bogart, Jose Ferrer, Van Johnson, and Fred McMurray. In addition to rare footage of the famed Firefall, the film featured horseback riding at the hotel, and breakfast being served on the patio outside the Presidential Suite (an amenity not actually offered at The Ahwahnee).

Paula Zahn and Harry Smith of *CBS This Morning* broadcast live from the hotel's Great Lounge the day after Mother's Day in 1994. The live television broadcast interspersed with taped segments (filmed earlier in the week) ran from 4 A.M. to 6 A.M. Though it was completely dark outside, a lighting crew made it look like dawn.

"The Ahwahnee is designed quite frankly for people who know the delights of luxurious living, and to whom the artistic excellence and the material comforts of their environment is important." —FROM AN EARLY AHWAHNEE ADVERTISEMENT

Such uncivilized behavior has long been anathema at The Ahwahnee. When Herbert Hoover, an avid outdoorsman and future president of the United States, visited the hotel, he ran afoul of a doorman who took him to task for attempting to enter the establishment in his fishing attire. Red Skelton found the stiff snobbishness at the hotel somewhat overdone; rankled by the dining room's strict dress code, he reportedly showed up to eat in a coat and tie, but no shirt.

Several members of the Star Trek crew, including Captain James T. Kirk and his Vulcan sidekick Spock (aka William Shatner and Leonard Nimoy) were beamed into the hotel during the filming of *Star Trek IV* in the park. Years later, Patrick Stewart, Shatner's successor in the role as Captain of the *Enterprise* for the series *The Next Generation*, stopped in as well. Mel Gibson made The Ahwahnee his home while shooting portions of the film *Maverick*.

Robert Redford actually worked at The Ahwahnee before launching his acting career. An ardent conservationist and producer of the highly acclaimed film, *Yosemite — The Fate of Heaven*, he has strong ties to Yosemite.

Other Hollywood stars who were guests at the hotel include Jack Benny, Shirley Temple Black, Bing Crosby, Charlton Heston, Douglas Fairbanks, Jr., Boris Karloff, and others.

A number of noted musicians have enjoyed the hotel's hospitality, and some have tested its storied acoustics. Marian Anderson checked in for a televised performance from Glacier Point in 1959, while soprano Anna Maria Alberghetti and tenor John McCormick were also guests. Folk singer Joan Baez provided a memorable impromptu performance of "Amazing Grace" at a Sunday brunch, and singer/songwriter John Fogerty of Creedence Clearwater Revival surprised guests at a wedding in the hotel when he produced an acoustic guitar and launched into an "unplugged" set of his classic hits accompanied by a harpist!

Heavy-metal band Metallica amazed The Ahwahnee kitchen staff with their appetite for foie gras and caviar. The kitchen, in turn, delighted rocker Bob Seeger, who found that the chef had carved the carrots accompanying his entrée into miniature Les Paul guitars.

Members of the San Francisco 49ers football organization, including Carmen Policy, Steve Young, and Bill Walsh, have huddled at the hotel. Seven-foot NBA star Bill Walton didn't stay at the hotel, though he did make

Future U.S. president Herbert Hoover was a Yosemite booster and frequent guest at The Ahwahnee. An avid outdoorsman, Hoover sponsored the Yosemite Winter Club's "Hoover Cup" awarded to the winner of the annual winter intercollegiate games. He is pictured here in 1927 with (from left) Superintendent W. B. Lewis, Hoover's wife, Donald and Mary Tressider.

a big impression when he stopped in for a bite to eat. Witnesses recall that the dimensions of the dining room fit him nicely, but he had to sit sideways because he couldn't fit his knees under the table.

The hotel has come a long way since Donald Tresidder, complaining about campers cutting through the hotel grounds, wrote that, "Many of our guests said they felt like museum exhibits to have a steady stream of people passing through the hotel." Agreeably, the social conceit of the hotel's early days seems to have given way to a much more appropriate feeling of casual elegance.

The crew of *Star Trek IV*, including Leonard Nimoy (pictured as a hovering Vulcan lieutenant Spock), drew a crowd while filming at Tunnel View. Stars William Shatner, Nimoy, and others made The Ahwahnee their base of operations during the project. Photograph by Lisa Strong-Aufhauser.

ABOVE
Challenging weather during Queen Elizabeth's visit in March of 1983 closed roads and kept curious onlookers to a minimum. In essence, the queen and duke had Yosemite to themselves, and the Yosemite community had the exclusive company of the royal party. Photograph by Michael Dixon, courtesy of DNC.

BELOW
Interpreter Julia Parker spent an entire year weaving the gift basket that she presented to Queen Elizabeth II and Prince Philip on behalf of the National Park Service and all California Native Americans. Initially intimidated by the idea of weaving a basket for her Royal Majesty, Julia concluded that it was the perfect gift. "The queen represents centuries of tradition. Likewise, our basket making represents centuries of tradition."

A ROYAL HOLIDAY

It was Saturday, March 5, 1983, and all Yosemite awaited the arrival of two of its most distinguished guests ever, Her Majesty, Queen Elizabeth II, and His Royal Highness, Prince Philip, Duke of Edinburgh.

The morning was gray and soggy, and not a single guest was registered at The Ahwahnee (due to security concerns, all reservations for rooms during the royal stay were rescheduled). Staff members were everywhere, their uniforms pressed and shoes polished. To honor the arriving guests, the Union Jack, symbol of Great Britain, was unfurled beneath the American flag.

The safety of the queen was of paramount concern and required close coordination between YP&CCo. and NPS officials, the United States Secret Service, the State Department, and the White House; state and local law enforcement agencies were also involved. By the time Her Majesty arrived, the hotel's only occupants were security personnel, including a "bomb-sniffer" dog that conducted thorough advance inspections of any facility the queen visited.

The weather proved to be mixed blessing during the visit. Rain almost turning to snow fell off and on throughout the weekend stay, dampening the scene and obscuring some of the landmarks. The inhospitable conditions kept curious onlookers to a minimum, so in many regards, the queen and duke had Yosemite to themselves, and the Yosemite community had the exclusive company of the royal party.

Former Superintendent Robert Binnewies recalled the moment when he and his assistant William Bergen greeted Her Majesty at Discovery View below the Wawona Tunnel. "It was remarkably quiet. There was a slight breeze blowing and the thunder of Bridalveil Fall was barely audible. A set of bleachers was erected in the parking lot to accommodate a press corps of over one hundred media representatives. They all were silent as the motorcade pulled to a stop. The moment the queen stepped out of the car, the bleachers erupted with the whir of camera motor drives. To this day I've never heard anything like it again."

The motorcade then proceeded to The Ahwahnee, where the queen and duke made a subdued entrance with little media fanfare. The only excitement was generated by the crowd that formed when the hotel elevator was unable to keep pace with the arriving entourage, "so there was much scurrying up the stairs."

Her Majesty and the duke made themselves at home on the hotel's sixth floor, which was entirely reserved for the royal party, including a footman, page, maid, and lady-in-waiting. Almost all the queen and duke's meals were personally prepared to order by The Ahwahnee chef, Marinus DeBruin, and his wife in the small kitchen off what is now the Mary Curry Tresidder Suite.

As if on cue, the park showed off its true beauty on Sunday morning. The clouds retreated, revealing a deep blue sky set against snow-clad peaks. In honor of the queen's visit, two services were scheduled at Yosemite's historic chapel. The first was for a select group of locals, who assembled in the crisp air outside the chapel afterwards to await the arrival of the queen and her party by bus for the second service.

Upon conclusion of the second service, the queen and duke emerged from the chapel amid another flurry of camera motor drives. Michael and Jeanne Adams, son and daughter-in-law of Ansel Adams, then presented the royals with an original Ansel Adams photograph entitled "Clearing Winter Storm," and Julia Parker, Yosemite's preeminent basketmaker, offered the visitors a beautiful gift basket that had taken her nearly a year to complete.

The Yosemite vacation was apparently the duke's idea, and the schedule was deliberately informal. A knowledgeable botanist and birder, he was eager to discuss international conservation and to ramble among the valley's massive ponderosa pines, despite the weather. As the rest of the entourage climbed into the waiting vehicles after a group walk around Mirror Lake with NPS interpreter Ginger Burley, he announced that he would rather hike back to the hotel. So off he went with ranger Burley, continuing the conversation about his work to save the endangered Asian ibis, secret servicemen slogging along at a discreet distance.

Dinner that evening was in The Ahwahnee dining room. A circular table for twelve was set in the alcove for the queen, duke, and a select group that included Superintendent Binnewies and his wife,

YP&CCo. president Ed Hardy and his wife, the U.S. Chief of Protocol, Selwa Roosevelt, and her husband, Archibald, the grandson of Teddy Roosevelt. Adjacent tables accommodated the rest of the entourage, and, to help provide a more intimate atmosphere in the immensity of the dining room, additional tables were set for families of the company's executive staff.

While the duke entertained his side of the table with lively conversation, the queen "held court" with the others, engaging in a quiet discussion about life in the park. Binnewies was struck by the queen's gentle personality and genuine interest in Yosemite and its residents. "She seemed delighted to spend extra time in the park. The weather had given her space and she appeared to recognize how unusual it was to have Yosemite to herself."

As the queen and duke prepared to leave the following day, Superintendent Binnewies, Ed and Jackie Hardy, Chef DeBruin and his wife, Sylvia, and Ahwahnee manager John O'Neill and wife Karen were summoned for private audiences. To each in turn, the royal couple expressed gratitude for efforts on their behalf and presented a leather-framed color photograph of themselves as a souvenir of the visit.

For the royals' departure, the staff lined both sides of the hotel lobby. The queen smiled radiantly and the employees burst into applause as Ed Hardy escorted her to the waiting limousine.

CHANGING TIMES,
CHANGING PHILOSOPHIES

If Stephen Mather had been worried about attracting sufficient numbers of park visitors when he first envisioned the hotel, his fears were proven unwarranted after World War II. Yosemite visitation boomed in the first three postwar decades, doubling every ten years. Attendance at the park was 641,000 in 1946, more than a million in 1956, and more than two million in 1967. The exponential growth couldn't be sustained, but in 1996, over four million travelers found their way to the park.

The Ahwahnee rode this wave of growing park popularity, and the company worked to meet the challenge of retaining the hotel's splendid atmosphere in the face of ever-increasing crowds. Beginning in the 1950s, the hotel settled into a pattern marked by high occupancy rates and few major changes.

The Ahwahnee's managers, while operating within the confines of a historic structure, have strived to adapt to the shifting use patterns and tastes of its guests. Most changes to the hotel have been operational, though some structural alterations have occurred. In 1950, Jeannette Dyer Spencer recommended that the original porte cochère, enclosed for use as a storage area by the Navy, be reopened for dancing, meeting, and cocktails and called the Indian Room. The concept was approved, and the room is now known as the Ahwahnee Lounge.

When the new Village Store was constructed in 1959, The Ahwahnee's beauty and barber shops were moved into that facility, freeing up space in the hotel. The former barber shop behind the registration desk and switchboard became an office, and the former beauty shop on the mezzanine became the manager's office. The former manager's office was converted to guest use as room 118.

New fire codes and safety concerns in the 1950s also dictated change. The "fireproof" hotel needed an extensive fire alarm system and exterior fire escape. In 1963, the elevator, which had always featured an operator, was automated, and in 1964 a modest, circular swimming pool was installed.

By the late 1960s, dining preferences were changing as well. In earlier years, a clientele made up of less active and often elderly guests favored the elaborate three daily meals included with a room under the American plan, notes historian Shirley Sargent. But younger, diet-and-exercise-conscious guests found that there was just too much food, and they didn't appreciate paying for a lunch that they missed while off hiking, bicycling, and otherwise enjoying the park. The Ahwahnee switched to the European plan in 1969.

Changing Fortunes

The death of Mary Curry Tresidder in her sixth-floor apartment in 1970 marked the end of the Curry family's control of the Yosemite Park & Curry Company. In a flurry of purchases and sales, YP&CCo. changed hands three times in just four years, beginning with the surreptitious acquisition of a large block of Curry stock by Shasta Telecasting Corporation.

The first two purchasers of the company (the capital-challenged Shasta Corporation and, in 1971, U.S. Natural Resources) were underfunded and unable to carry out even routine maintenance of the diverse concession facilities. To reduce overhead, many long-time employees, including Jeannette and Ted Spencer, were pressured to leave.

During this period of revolving door ownership, the character of the hotel nearly underwent a dramatic change. Seeking to offset the loss in revenue and rooms that occurred when the historic Glacier Point Hotel burned in 1969, the new managers explored construction of replacement facilities in Yosemite Valley. The plan they considered to be the most advantageous was to build additional one- and two-story, mid-priced cottages on the grounds of The Ahwahnee. The planners forecast that the eventual overnight capacity for the hotel and its outlying units would increase from 250 beds to 1,000!

Limited by the 1971 buying power of the $600,000 insurance award for the Glacier Point Hotel, however, the concessioner was unable to afford the proposed new facilities (that featured ghastly designs), and they were never built.

In August 1973, U.S. Natural Resources sold the Yosemite contract to MCA, Inc.—an entertainment conglomerate originally known as Music Corporation of America—for $13 million.

At the time MCA took over, The Ahwahnee was nearing its 50th anniversary and beginning to show signs of neglect. MCA's executives hired Edward C. Hardy to be their chief operating officer in Yosemite. Hardy accepted the job with the provision that significant funding be allocated for the rehabilitation of The Ahwahnee and other lodging units. MCA met his request by committing $2,000,000 for a major program of improvement, including the replacement of boilers, an exterior renovation, and restoration of the interior decor.

Over the next twenty years, various components of the hotel were completely disassembled and restored, or replaced. San Francisco architect Walter Sontheimer was commissioned to oversee work on the exterior, and designer Marian Van Tress oversaw the interior decoration. Among other problems, the valley's weather, with alternately freezing and thawing temperatures, combined with poor maintenance to cause the deterioration of the faux wood beams on the exterior of the hotel. The concrete crumbled, exposing the steel understructure. Architect Sontheimer recommended enclosing the beams in transparent fiberglass sleeves that would retard and contain any future degeneration.

ABOVE
The famous Beacon or "Sleepy Hollow" chairs of the Great Lounge date from the hotel's opening. They seem to be designed with this room in mind, for the reclined attitude of the chairs angles the eyes of their occupants toward the beautiful stencils on the ceiling.

ABOVE
Two tennis courts were added to the grounds of the hotel in 1928. To publicize the addition, an inaugural tournament featuring name players was organized. Following the hotel management's early and unsuccessful attempts to offer dancing on the sixth floor and mezzanine of The Ahwahnee, the courts also served as an outside dance pavilion as late as 1941.

ABOVE MIDDLE
Jeannette Dyer Spencer and Mary Curry Tresidder scoured the foothills of California's gold country to locate authentic props to decorate the El Dorado Diggins Bar as a "Wild West" town. Photograph by Ansel Adams, YP&CCo. Collection.

TOP
As one enters The Ahwahnee, a pedestal to the right of the door supports a granite slab with a plaque that commemorates the hotel's inclusion on the National Register of Historic Landmarks on June 2, 1987. This entrance is technically the side entrance. The hotel's architect, Gilbert Stanley Underwood, had intended that guests enter from the doors just inside and to the left, which now lead to The Ahwahnee Lounge.

ABOVE
With a fireplace, paneled walls, and original leaded windows, the Tresidder Library is one of the hotel's most memorable rooms. When the ill-conceived sixth-floor ballroom was eventually sectioned off, this room became part of Mary and Donald Tresidder's private residence. An oil portrait of Donald Tresidder hangs in the suite that must be rented along with the adjoining guest room.

The guest rooms were updated for the 50th anniversary as well. In the name of comfort and efficiency, cast iron radiators were exchanged for thermostatically-controlled steam heaters. Every window, too, was replaced, and dark-framed screens were installed to foil the ring-tailed cats that routinely climbed in the windows to gather various garments from guest rooms to pad their nests.

The El Dorado Diggins bar, which was used less and less as a private dining room or bar, was transformed into a guest suite. The storefronts and historic decorations that gave the pub its "Old West" feel were carefully stored away until the hotel's most recent renovation in the late 1990s.

On the grounds of the hotel, a wildflower trail was added, and the nine-hole golf course and chain-link fence were removed in response to changing environmental sensitivities; the sprinkler system was retained to irrigate the grounds and continue service as fire protection.

Historic Designation

All the efforts to spruce up the hotel paid off, for on February 15, 1977, The Ahwahnee was nominated to the National Register of Historic Landmarks. A plaque commemorating the listing is situated just outside the lobby doors. The NPS thematic architectural study states, "The principal significance of The Ahwahnee lies in its monumental rustic architecture. Inseparable from that architecture is the period art work and interior design so carefully executed throughout the building."

Major renovation projects continued well beyond the 1977 anniversary. Eleven years later, the wooden porte cochère that serves as the hotel's entrance was replaced. Built of logs two feet in circumference, it was completely disassembled and reconstructed exactly as before, this time using Douglas fir instead of sugar pine to meet current snow-load specifications.

Around the same time, the hotel's slate roof was painstakingly replaced. Following the architect's original specifications for color and grade, workers swapped each tile, weighing 1-1/4 pounds, for a new one, obtained from the same Vermont quarry used for the original roof. The process took over four years to complete.

During the queen's visit in 1983, televisions were moved temporarily onto the hotel's sixth floor. It was not until 1989, however, that televisions were installed throughout the hotel. A year later, the guest rooms got a little more comfortable when the hotel's passive ventilation scheme—which had been drastically altered when the transoms above the doors of the guest rooms were sealed to meet changing fire codes—was replaced with a high-velocity air-conditioning system.

Given the many changes to the operational aspects of the building, it is surprising how many of the original furnishings still exist from when the hotel opened in 1927. The fabrics have changed to keep pace with contemporary trends, but most of the tables, chairs, and sofas have served guests in The Ahwahnee's public areas since day one.

The first wedding held in The Ahwahnee took place in the Solarium just two weeks after the hotel opened in 1927. With its five immense windows framing the oak woodland and soaring granite cliffs, the room, described by the hotel's original decorator as "a sheltered bit of the outdoors," continues to be the most popular site for wedding receptions and private parties.

The Ahwahnee has three grand pianos, two of which are Steinways. The "tiger mahogany" instrument is a vintage 1902 Model "C". The other Steinway is a nine-foot ebony Model "D" that was purchased for the hotel in April of 1927. It was at the center of a famous Ahwahnee moment in January of 1947, when management reportedly interrupted an impromptu, late-night concert by Judy Garland, attended by Lucille Ball and Desi Arnaz.

THE NAVY CHECKS IN

"No patient at this hospital has any real cause to complain of lack of recreation. Sufficient variety and amount is available to all."

—CAPTAIN REYNOLDS HAYDEN, (MC) USN

From June 23, 1943 to December 15, 1945, The Ahwahnee was closed to the public, and commissioned as the U.S. Naval Convalescent Hospital, Yosemite National Park. The hotel was just one of many resort-area properties drafted into service during the early years of the war to help ease the anticipated burden that battle casualties would place on existing naval hospitals. The temporary hospitals included Sun Valley Lodge in Idaho, Glenwood Springs, Colorado, and Arrowhead Springs in San Bernardino, California.

The Ahwahnee was initially pegged as an ideal location to send battle-stressed patients awaiting discharge or reassignment. Once it began operation as a hospital, however, this use proved to be a poor one. Bureaucratic backlogs in Washington, D.C., turned what were supposed to be brief visits into lengthy ones that seemed like prison stays to the sailors. The early patients apparently found the high cliffs claustrophobic and the isolation unbearable.

By the time the war ended, patients at the hospital had become predominantly medical and surgical cases. For these servicemen, the park's natural beauty was inspiring, and the hospital offered multiple occupational and recreational activities.

Anchors Aweigh
The hotel closed its doors to the public on May, 30, 1943, the same day that the Navy's first representative, maintenance officer Lieutenant Will Grimes, arrived. More staff appeared dur-

ing the first week of June, the hospital was officially commissioned on June 25, 1943, and the first patients arrived a week later.

The Navy calculated that given sufficient lavatory facilities, they could squeeze as many as 1,000 patients into the hotel (853 was the maximum actually achieved). Over 80 of those patients were expected to reside in the Great Lounge, which was converted to Ward A. A large bathhouse for this group constructed just west of the lounge and solarium became the first in a series of temporary buildings constructed to meet the needs of the hospital.

Other modifications clearly communicated the changed nature of the hotel. A fence with a cap of barbed wire was constructed around the perimeter of the 36-acre compound, a small guard house was built by the entrance lobby, and a two-cell brig was erected in the parking lot.

The inside of the hotel proved readily adaptable to the Navy's needs. Guest rooms served a variety of uses, from dental offices to X-ray labs, with most used as wards. Enlisted men housed in guest rooms rather than the Great Lounge shared space with nine others assigned to spots on five sets of bunk beds. Officers enjoyed slightly better conditions, with single beds and half as many room occupants.

While originally occupied by nurses, the sixth-floor penthouse became the commanding officer's quarters. Nurses were moved to the fifth floor. The fourth floor was reserved for officers, the third housed officers and enlisted men as needed, and the second floor was a mixture of labs and wards. Administrative offices were concentrated on the mezzanine. On the ground floor, the hotel's original porte cochère was enclosed to store baggage, the gift shop became the personnel office, the sweet shop became the "ship store," the cloak room served as a post office, and the dining room became what was almost certainly the most beautiful mess hall in the entire Navy.

The transformation that was most notable, however, was of the Diggins Bar, which with some clever craftsmanship became the Catholic chapel. The sanctuary lamp was fashioned from a pickle jar and the top of a cocktail shaker with a hand-made frame to hold them. The altar was built over the bar counter, and the former rustic bar-rail became the communion rail. Not to be outdone, a Protestant chaplain subsequently oversaw the construction of a second altar for his own worshippers in the Mural Room, which had housed three pool tables until a separate pool hall was constructed in 1945.

Rough Waters

While the hospital was well adapted for its mission by war's end, patients and staff suffered significantly from lack of adequate supplies and unrealistic expectations the first two years of operation. One commentator noted that "conditions at the hospital in Yosemite could almost be described as desperate" during that time.

Support and improvements came slowly and rarely from the Naval authorities in Washington, D.C. Fortunately, the hospital was adopted by the people of the San Joaquin Valley: the Army in

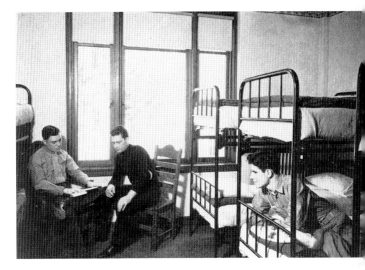

TOP
Beginning in December of 1943, Navy officials worked to install bowling alleys at the hotel as recreational outlets for hospital patients. It took six months to acquire a building, and six months more passed before The Bay Meadows race track and California Jockey Club donated $5,000 to buy the lanes. A bowling league was formed with matches four nights a week.

ABOVE
Guest rooms of The Ahwahnee—small by contemporary standards—were stuffed with double-tier bunk beds by the Navy. Overnight capacity for the hotel and cottages today is roughly 250 guests. Accustomed to housing sailors in the tight confines aboard ship, the Navy figured that 900 to 1,000 could live in the building for extended periods!

PREVIOUS PAGE
A group of sailors awaiting discharge from the U.S. Naval Convalescent Hospital in Yosemite takes in the sights of Yosemite Valley from the Four Mile Trail.

TOP
A 1943 picture of the hotel lobby highlights changes in the area now occupied by the concierge desk. The wall behind the officer on the left is the former exterior wall of the Sweet Shop. What is now a lounge area was once part of the shop. Scars on the concrete floor between the columns and adjacent to the concierge desk define the former walls, which were removed to make better use of the space when the hotel reopened following the Navy occupation between 1943 and 1946.

ABOVE
Navy brass viewed The Ahwahnee as an ideal location to convalesce for soldiers awaiting medical discharge. Bureaucratic backlogs combined with the remote nature and high walls of the Yosemite Valley, however, agitated the patients. By the time it was decommissioned in the summer of 1945, the hospital had been greatly improved and was replete with the latest medical equipment and a wide array of recreational opportunities. It provided occupational therapy, "better than most and second to none in service hospitals."

Merced and Fresno; the San Joaquin Valley Elks, Navy Club, and War Dads of Fresno; the Navy Mother's Clubs; and Veterans of Foreign Wars.

Rest and Relaxation

Captain Reynolds Hayden, the hospital's commanding officer, recognized that in order to maintain good morale, it was essential that there be plenty of recreational activities for patients. He issued a standing offer to feed and house anyone who made the trip to entertain the hospital's residents. The first professional entertainment was provided by patriotic corporations, and included the Shell Oil Co. Show and Reynolds Tobacco Company's Camel Caravan. As well, hostesses and orchestras were brought to the hospital from the San Joaquin Valley for dances.

The hospital eventually even had its own band, the Yosemite Rhythm Kings, which performed at dances and special functions. Though the cast was ever-changing, a nucleus from the hospital staff managed to keep the music flowing.

Physical activity, whether it was dancing or recreational competition, was vital to the speedy recovery of injured servicemen. Therapists worked with 100 to 150 sailors for as many as three one-hour sessions per day. Outdoor recreation supplemented the hands-on physical therapy.

When the hospital originally opened, patients looking for outdoor recreation could choose from the "hazardous" 800-yard pitch-and-putt golf course, horseshoes, tennis, and softball. Supervised hikes were led three times each week, and bikes and horses could be rented through YP&CCo. Later a concrete pad was poured for combination tennis, basketball, and handball courts. Shuffleboard, volleyball, croquet, and badminton courts were also laid out.

Badger Pass ski area was especially popular with staff and patients eager to get out of the confines of Yosemite Valley during winter. Groups were transported to the slopes in flatbed trucks outfitted with wooden benches and canvas tops. Those who survived the ride found the skiing somewhat challenging: five broken legs were reported the first two weeks. A program of instruction was quickly established, and the worst subsequent injury was a sprained ankle.

By the time the hospital ceased service, indoor facilities had grown to include a recreation hall seating 400 where movies were shown five nights a week, a pool hall with eight pool tables and one billiard table, and a weight room. The most popular attraction was the six Brunswick bowling alleys purchased new with $5,000 donated by the California Jockey Club at Bay Meadows race track. Bowling leagues were established, pitting ward against ward and officers against enlisted men.

Perhaps the biggest recreational advance at the hospital occurred in April of 1945, when the Secretary of the Navy authorized beer sales in the ship's store. The Yosemite naval hospital became the only one in the United States to earn that distinction. This was not a perk the sailors took for granted. Reports have it that 1,000 to 1,500 pints of beer were sold each night.

Rehabilitation

Hospital administrators also worked hard to prepare the sailors for life after the war. Patients at the hospital could take courses in math, language (including Chinese, Russian, Spanish, and French), electronics, mechanics, fly tying, weaving, leatherwork, woodwork, printing, bookbinding, plastics, sheetmetal, ceramics, lapidary, jewelry design, and more. A donation of books by Fresno State students was the start of a library collection, and within six months, it had mushroomed to 3,500 volumes in the three rooms that now constitute the Presidential Suite.

Though the hospital got off to a shaky start, the majority of the 6,752 patients who were treated during its tenure left with a tremendous sense of appreciation for the time they spent there. When the hospital was decommissioned in December of 1945, outgoing staff could look back with pride on their accomplishments, as well.

Back to Work

The transition from hospital back to hotel was not so nearly so swift as had been hoped. Damage to the building and its grounds was significant. "Sailors had banged holes in walls, torn boards off closets, damaged the chests, and gouged floors," writes Shirley Sargent. YP&CCo. estimates

were that it would take $250,000 to return the hotel to its pre-hospital state. Jeannette Dyer Spencer and her husband Ted oversaw the repairs and refurbishment that began April 30, 1946. Their target for reopening was Christmas of the same year.

Progress was steady, with almost no major problems and only a few tense moments. A fire in the carpentry shop could have been much worse, and a blast from the demolition crew taking down the Navy recreation hall broke one of the plate glass windows in the dining room. Priority work was completed on schedule, and the hotel hosted a reopening party for locals, where several modifications were debuted.

For returning guests, the most significant change was a new design element. A large, Mondrian-style, geometric mural was painted over the fireplace on the north wall of the Great Lounge by Jeannette and Ted's daughter, Frann Spencer Reynolds. At the same time the complex stencils which originally decorated the room's beams were painted over. This may have been a cost-saving measure, though it's more likely this step was taken to provide an uncluttered visual environment for the new mural.

When the trumpet fanfare announced the start of the hastily-organized Bracebridge Dinner on December 25, the war and its challenges were just memories, and once again The Ahwahnee resumed its place as the premier hotel in the national park system.

The term "public area" took on greater meaning during the Navy occupation of the hotel when the comfortable confines of the Great Lounge were transformed into "Ward A," housing approximately one hundred patients in four rows of double-tier bunk beds. Commanding officers occupied the sixth-floor apartments, nurses quarters were on the fifth floor, and convalescing officers filled the fourth. Enlisted men were housed on the first, second, and third floors. With limited recreational activities and cramped living conditions, the soldiers had few fond memories of their stay in Yosemite's premier hotel.

6,752 patients were treated at the hospital between May 30, 1943 and December 15, 1945, peaking with 853 at one time. When the war ended, company managers found they had new battles to fight. The hotel had suffered significant damage during the hospital years. It took a full year and $400,000 to restore the building and heavily-impacted grounds.

A NEW ERA OF STEWARDSHIP

In 1993 the contract for running concessions in Yosemite was awarded to Delaware North Companies (DNC), a privately held firm headquartered in Buffalo, New York. Though the company had no previous experience running hotels in national parks, DNC had prospered providing quality, high-volume food service in sports venues, and its bid emphasized a commitment to upgrade the park's facilities and services.

DNC's subsidiary, Yosemite Concession Services (YCS) commenced operation in Yosemite on October 1, 1993. It was a revolutionary 15-year contract, for DNC agreed to purchase YP&CCo.'s possessory interest in the buildings and then turn them over to the National Park Service. The company also agreed to give approximately 20 percent of its annual revenues to the government for addition to a "capital improvement fund."

As a result of this new arrangement, The Ahwahnee would no longer be an asset of the corporate entity that managed the hotel. Instead, at the end of the 15-year contract, it would belong to the American people. Money from the capital improvement fund would be used to maintain the hotel.

Within two years, YCS, which changed its name to DNC Parks & Resorts at Yosemite in 2003, launched a comprehensive $1.5 million remodel of guest rooms, public areas, and gift shop at The

Ahwahnee. Under the direction of Becky Chambers of Chambers/Lorenz Design Associates of Fresno, California, the guest rooms were brightened with specially-designed headboards, storage chests, and armoires, and an array of custom fabrics used for bedspreads, upholstery, and window treatments.

Historic photographs were added as decorative and interpretive design elements. For example, the guest rooms and suites on the sixth floor of the hotel, formerly the residence of Donald and Mary Tresidder, were hung with photographs of the couple to approximate the feeling of a private residence.

TOP
The walls of the lounge adjacent to the Sweet Shop are decorated with original watercolors by Swedish artist Gunnar Widforss.

ABOVE
The interiors of The Ahwahnee cottages continue the Native American theme of the main building through stenciled details and fabric choices.

ABOVE
The Ahwahnee Gift Shop originally featured "gifts from around the world," but the selection of merchandise today is more regional. The shop was refurbished in 1998 by San Francisco designer Linda Wong, who added the colorful linoleum Ahwahnee logo in the floor and augmented the room's historic pendant lamps with low-wattage halogen lamps to provide a brighter, friendlier appearance.

FAR RIGHT
The Ahwahnee Gift Shop features a "signature" line of Ahwahnee merchandise, including beautiful and distinctive apparel, monogrammed with the classic Ahwahnee, three-legged Indian logo designed by Jeannette Dyer Spencer.

A display of turquoise jewelry in The Ahwahnee Gift Shop.

BELOW
Four hundred tons of slate, obtained from the same quarry in Vermont used in The Ahwahnee's 1927 construction, were purchased in 2003 to re-roof the hotel.

Oversize portraits of historic Yosemite figures, from John Muir to Chief Lemee, grace the walls of the Great Lounge, while the Solarium features photographs of sketches of early hotel furnishings by Gunnar Widforss. Two large wrought iron table lamps on the seventeenth-century-style tables in the lounge were inspired by the hotel's chandeliers. Commissioned for the remodel, the lamps simultaneously add light and draw one's eyes toward the ceiling.

San Francisco designer Linda Wong was selected to update the gift shop, which sells a "signature" line of Ahwahnee merchandise, original artwork, and handcrafts. By the integration of small, low-wattage halogen lamps with the building's original iron-and-glass pendant light fixtures, the shop was brightened. Taking inspiration from the mosaics in the lobby, the shop's floor was revamped with new linoleum and a color inlay of The Ahwahnee's "three-legged Indian" logo.

Environmental Awareness
DNC managers realize that The Ahwahnee provides excellent opportunities to demonstrate the viability of ecologically-sensitive products and management practices without sacrificing quality in the guest experience. For instance, the compact fluorescent lights that replaced the incandescent bulbs in the hotel had no negative impact on hotel illumination levels, but they save over 10,000 watts of electricity daily.

A related development was the use of a revolutionary new replacement carpet in the hotel hallways. Custom woven for The Ahwahnee, the carpeting blends with the historic character of the hotel, using The Ahwahnee logo and color scheme in its design. What makes the carpet special is that it is composed of recycled materials that can be recycled again when the carpet eventually wears out.

A Diamond in the Wilderness

Old black-and-white images of the newly-opened hotel portray a massive stone and timber castle amid barren grounds, the sheer cliffs of Yosemite a stark backdrop. The pictures reveal a newly-completed building that tries to, but does not quite blend with its environment. As the carefully-selected plants and trees have matured over the years, the facility now seems to be part of its surroundings, rather than just in them.

In July of 2002, The Ahwahnee marked its diamond anniversary. While the hotel is seventy-five years old, there are other properties in the national parks that are older and bigger. Still, none so successfully combine high art and rustic beauty in such a supreme setting. Over three-quarters of a century, the hotel has served as a peaceful, inspirational oasis despite floods, rockfalls, fires, world wars, and government shutdowns. It unfailingly provides the restorative energy that its creators envisioned in the midst of the park's splendor.

The Ahwahnee's very first registered guest on opening day, July 14, 1927, was NPS Director Stephen T. Mather himself. As he strolled through the magnificent public areas after signing in, he no doubt felt complete satisfaction that his dream of a first-rate hotel in Yosemite had been realized. His dream lives on today.

TOP
The grounds of The Ahwahnee were originally landscaped by Carl Purdy of Ukiah, California, under the direction of noted architect Fredrick Law Olmsted, Jr. The sequoia (foreground) was planted about 1886 by George W. Kenney, the founder of Kenneyville, a settlement that once occupied the hotel grounds.

INSET
The reflecting pond adjacent to the port cochére was added in 1931 to "reflect the cliffs and trees of Yosemite" and to provide visual interest for the "back" of the hotel.

The alcove window of The Ahwahnee dining room was designed to frame a view of Yosemite Falls for diners. On a snowy winter morning, the alcove itself is a beautiful sight, embodying "park rustic" architecture at its best.